THE PINE CONE RANCH

It appeared to be murder without reason when someone bushwhacked the foreman of the Pine Cone cow outfit. But there was a reason, an involved and bitter one ... Pine Cone's owner, rugged and stubborn Jake Beam, hired a new rider, Sam Bolt, and that was when trouble really started. But for Jake Beam, the simple matter of avenging his slain rangeboss turned into a nightmare he never could have imagined, and for Sam Bolt it turned into a kind of personal danger he did not expect, but could not walk away from. The result was unparalleled for them both.

THE PINE CONE RANCH

John Hunt

A Lythway Book

CHIVERS PRESS
BATH

First published in Great Britain 1985
by
Robert Hale Limited
This Large Print edition published by
Chivers Press
by arrangement with
Robert Hale Limited
1987

ISBN 0 7451 0455 X

© Robert Hale Limited 1985

British Library Cataloguing in Publication Data

Hunt, John, *1916—*
    The Pine Cone Ranch.—Large print ed.
    —(A Lythway book)
    Rn: Lauran Paine I. Title
    813'.54[F]   PS3566.A34

ISBN 0–7451–0455–X

THE PINE CONE RANCH

CHAPTER ONE

CHARLEY WHITSON

It was no small accomplishment because the Pine Cone covered thirty thousand acres of territory, from the westerly mountains and piney-woods foothills to the undulating grasslands over beyond the town of Rochester almost within shouting distance of the railroad siding outside of Kerville, without so much as a drift fence on any of it; therefore horses, which are by instinct running animals, were hard to find, harder to drive, and next to impossible to herd toward the home-place and into the large old network of pole corrals. But they did it, and even more admirable, they did it all in one day.

The hands were putting up their using animals and Charley Whitson was approaching the tie-rack out front of the huge old log horse-barn, pulling off his gloves and faintly smiling in the direction of his employer, Jake Beam, when the gunshot came out of nowhere and Charley went down like a pole-axed steer, and for ten seconds the stunned men inside the barn, and Mister Beam out front, were immobilised by the absolute impossibility of what had happened.

Then Mister Beam jumped ahead beside his fallen rangeboss and five riders charged forth from the barn, guns in hand, recklessly and furiously intent upon finding the bushwhacker.

They did not find him, even though the *cocinero* told them he had seen a horseman racing eastward about a half mile out, and even though they went in a flinging chase. But it required time to snake out fresh animals, rig them out and pile aboard in a rush out of the yard.

They found tracks. By the time they were within sight of town they had dozens of sets of shod-horse tracks.

Jake Beam had Charley laid out on his bed in the little foreman's room off the back of the bunkhouse, and by the time the men returned on tired horses, Jake had pretty well recovered. When they trooped up to the bunkhouse from the barn he had the lamp lighted and a bottle of whiskey on the bunkhouse table.

That little door in the back wall which led into the foreman's room was open. They could see Charley lying on his cot as though asleep. There was some blood, but not much. The bullet which had killed him had ploughed through from the left side of his upper body, and without hitting bone exited on the right side. During its course it had burst Charley Whitson's heart and collapsed both his lungs. Death had been so sudden and swift Charley had actually bled very little.

Jake Beam, a craggy, stocky, granite-jawed

2

man in his late sixties who had grey-blue, gunmetal-coloured eyes and sandy-rust-coloured hair, watched the five rangemen pour whiskey and said, 'Where did you lose him?'

Abel Carnes, the Pine Cone tophand, a lanky, taciturn, part-Indian looking man was raising his cup when he answered. 'Down near Rochester. Light was failing and there was tracks everywhere.' Abel drank and briefly ground his teeth, put the cup aside and also said, 'I don't know, Mister Beam. He either headed for town because that was where he figured to go anyway, or he went down there because he figured we'd lose his sign down there—and maybe he rode through town from the north end and out the south end, and is maybe still going ... He could do that; in the dark he could ride all night...'

Beam listened with his head lowered a little, his familiar stance while listening or thinking. A straw-headed rider with pale eyes and perpetually peeling, very fair face, said, 'Why? He planned that right careful. Countin' the cook there'd be seven men on his trail right after he pulled the trigger. He was hiding out yonder somewhere and seen us bring in the horses and all. He knew how many we was ... Why in the hell did he kill Charley in the first place? ... I think he had to hate him awful bad to bushwhack him right smack dab in the middle of the yard, knowin' all the hands was around.'

Mister Beam slowly poured whiskey then raised the thick white crockery cup and held it about even with his chest as he looked at them. He had been in the Portales country all his life. He had arrived there as a suckling in an old worn-out wagon behind two Mexican mules; his father had been a hide hunter. His maw had helped with the skinning. Sixty years of unsmiling hard labour, along with the natural growth of both the countryside and the eastern market for quality beef, had made Jacob Beam a wealthy landholder whose domain was adequate—and deeded.

He had not got there by being soft or very forgiving. His character like his disposition had hardened into what it was now. As he listened to Abel and the straw-haired man, whose name was Cotton Buford, he ranged a grey-hard gaze around until it settled upon a dark-haired man with almost completely black eyes, who was slightly shorter than either Abel or Cotton, and said, 'What do you think, Morales?'

The thick-shouldered, short-backed man considered the contents of his cup while replying. 'They were new shoes. I think there'll be a lot of new horseshoes around Rochester.' The black eyes came up, their gaze non-committal. Morales shrugged.

Mister Beam sat down without touching the contents of his cup. Gradually, the others also sank down upon the benches on both sides of

4

the bunkhouse table. Mister Beam let go a long pent-up breath. 'It took me plumb by surprise. By gawd I could hardly believe it ... Charley ... What in the hell; he was taking off his gloves and walkin' toward me from the barn. By gawd—he was killed just like that...'

Beam's slaty grey-blue eyes went around the table. They stopped again upon the burly, short-backed man. 'Morales, first thing in the morning study out his sign as long as you can.'

Morales nodded.

Jake Beam's rugged countenance was troubled by exasperation. 'We need something. We need his tracks goin' to a particular house in town, or a particular camp somewhere. We need to know why he did it, then I expect we can figure out who he is.'

The tophand tipped back his hat. He was tired, it had been a long, arduous day, even before they'd all got strung out on empty bellies trying to find that son of a bitch. He said, 'I got an idea he didn't just come skulkin' out here this afternoon and got lucky. I got a notion he knew the yard, and maybe where we was and when we come back. And for a fact, he knew where to hide himself and his horse ... Tell you what: He's been scoutin' us up for a long time to be able to do it like he done—quick and easy, and get off clean afterwards.'

Jake Beam's tufted, gingery brows had dropped a notch during the tophand's comments. Now, he said, 'All right, Abel; what is your point?'

'That it ain't likely someone didn't notice a man on our range durin' the length of time it took that feller to learn all he had to know in order to bushwhack Charley neat as a whistle, then get clean away.'

Jake Beam finally lifted the cup and drank from it. Opposite him the straw-haired man drew forth a plug and worried off a corner of it, got his cud pouched into one cheek and returned the plug to a shirt pocket. Morales tipped a little more whiskey into his cup. His face was sweat-shiny in the lamplight. He was light tan coloured. He said, 'It was personal . . . If it had been against Pine Cone . . . You was a better target, Mister Beam, leaning on the rack out front, standin' still . . . He waited. If me or someone else had walked out, he would have kept on waiting until Charley walked out.' Morales' very dark eyes lifted.

They sat a while with their private speculations before Cotton Buford, the blond man, prefaced what he had to say with a sigh of resignation. 'I guess so . . . I guess the son of a bitch had it in for Charley, an' only Charley, and I guess like Abel said, he'd been plannin' for a while . . . Now then, I only been on Pine Cone a year. Charley was always decent with me, but some of you fellers knew him better. What did he do that made someone kill him like that?'

6

Mister Beam who had known the rangeboss best—and they all knew this—leaned both thick arms on the table. 'I don't know,' he muttered. 'I thought about that before you boys got back, when I was settin' on a chair in his room lookin' at him. I don't know. Charley's been with me almost eleven years. As far as I know he never done anything that'd make *me* that mad at him.' Mister Beam leaned back off the table. 'I don't think we'd ought to fret much about that anyway, because—well hell—every man's got private things about him. And maybe it was something from many years back. I'm going into town first thing in the morning and talk to Marshal Hedrich.' As he finished speaking and arose from the table, Mister Beam showed a faint, death's-head smile. 'I'll tell you what, boys, we're going to find that son of a bitch, and we're goin' to hang him wherever we come onto him.'

After Mister Beam left the bunkhouse for the main-house, a young rider, who had been silent during the time when Jake Beam had been in the bunkhouse, went to work rolling a cigarette as he quietly said, 'Maybe it's like he said. Maybe it was Charley that bastard was after.' He paused to light up before continuing. 'And maybe tomorrow while one of us is on the range, he'll kill another Pine Cone rider ... When I was a kid back in Missouri, it happened that way kind of often. Someone would be ridin' past

7

some trees, and get killed from ambush ...
Without no reason folks could figure out.' The
young rangeman looked straight at Abel Carnes.
'I'd like to draw my pay in the morning.'

That swung the thoughts of the others in a
fresh and unexpected direction. Abel, who was
not the foreman, just the tophand, looked
annoyedly at the quitting cowboy. 'Why didn't
you say something to Mister Beam when he was
in here?'

The cowboy spoke around his quirley. 'Just
didn't want to is all. You're the tophand, the
foreman's dead. You're next in line. You can tell
Mister Beam.' As he finished speaking the
cowboy arose and walked over to his dark corner
bunk and started peeling off to bed down.

A rider who wore boots with drover's heels
and who had one of those stiff-brimmed, low-
crowned hats began to wag his head a trifle
dolefully and kept his face down as he said, 'Me
too, Abel. I'm sorry. I been right fond of the
Pine Cone ranch for two years now, but I been
thinkin' like the kid; damned if I'm goin' to stay
here for some crazy bastard to shoot off my
horse ... I'd like my pay tomorrow too.'

The lanky tophand's expression reflected
troubled thoughts. As tophand, he had been a
straw-boss, but nothing more. Decisions he had
made had been purely functional ones. He was
not prepared for any of this, it upset him to
think of it, and in fact as good a stockman as he

was, Abel Carnes had all his mature life been avoiding any kind of serious and weighty responsibility.

He had never aspired to Charley Whitson's job. With a sweep of a sinewy arm he brought the crockery cup in close and hoisted it, then blinked back the water and looked across at Cotton and Morales; they gazed steadily back. Cotton dryly said, 'I rode my butt off today an' I'm tired.' He arose and hung there a moment ignoring the pair of men who had quit. 'Maybe tomorrow we find some sign of the son of a bitch.'

When Morales arose to head for his bunk he did not even say that much. 'I been shot at before, and didn't get hit.'

The last man to head for his bunk was Abel. He went over to stand in the doorway where he could see the dead rangeboss, and slowly closed the door, then blew down the lamp mantle and in the darkness went over to sit down on the side of his bunk to tug boots off swollen feet.

CHAPTER TWO

THE DAY AFTER

The *cocinero* was a pulpy older man with a limp and maybe fifty grey hairs which he grew long on one side, then swept up over his bald skull. He put food on the table for Mister Beam, Abel Carnes and Cotton Buford. The young cowboy and the older one had drawn their pay, got their private horses and were gone.

Morales was not there either. At Jake Beam's raised brows the *cocinero* said, 'He come in and rousted me out to make him up a bundle of grub then he rode out . . . How in the hell does a man read tracks in the dark, I'd like to know . . . Even a Messican.'

Mister Beam had a fork poised as he said, 'What did he say, Harold?'

'Nothing . . . Just that he wanted me to make him up a bundle. But he was wearin' his gun and shell-belt and had a carbine slung under his *rosadero*.'

'Riding a ranch horse?'

'Yes.'

Mister Beam went to work on his fried potatoes and morning steak. 'Then he didn't quit,' he stated.

They were out front of the barn with Abel looking as uncomfortable as he felt when Mister Beam asked them to lend him a hand rigging up the top-buggy, and during that time he told them to hang close to the yard until he got back from Rochester. There was no pressing need to do much today, anyway, although the reason they had brought in fresh horses was because the intention had been to start a gather within a

10

few days—after they'd shod the fresh animals and otherwise got ready for some serious and far-ranging saddlebacking.

But it could wait a few days. Springtime was passing but summer was not yet fully over the land. They could wait as long as a week, if they had to, and as Jake Beam drove out of the yard in the direction of town, he thought they would probably have to.

He'd had since late yesterday afternoon to adjust to events. He lit a cigar as the buggy horse trotted ahead and the morning sun gradually warmed things up. He was by nature a direct, very practical man without much humour or much softness. He was a widower; his wife had been a half-breed Ute woman who had died in childbirth many years earlier. Since then he'd had nothing to divert his attention from the Pine Cone cow outfit.

Over a half-century he had encountered his share of difficulties ranging from deadly droughts to even more merciless winter storms which buried livestock. He had done everything possible to survive conditions over which he had no control, but the ones over which he could exert some degree of control, such as losing cattle and horses to thieves, he had handled exactly in accordance with his nature: He had shot or hanged every one of them he and his riders had been able to catch.

Now, with the Rochester rooftops in sight,

his teeth were clamped around the cigar and his weathered, rugged countenance showed an unwavering degree of resolve.

He and Charley Whitson had been together for more than ten years, and even with a disposition which seemed to avoid close relationships, they had shared some good times and bad times. Jake Beam had been fond of his rangeboss. Nothing was going to prevent him from settling this matter the way it should be settled.

He left the rig at the barn below the stage depot at the lower end of town and walked up to the jailhouse where Marshal Tom Hedrich had his office. The building was old; much of Rochester had hidden log walls beneath planed wood siding, but the jailhouse looked like what it had once been; a tradingpost and fort. The roof was low, the walls were massive, all the windows and door stuck because the fir foundation logs had been rotting for years, and the entire structure sagged.

Tom Hedrich was a large man, better than six feet tall, and weighed slightly more than two hundred pounds. At one time, perhaps ten years earlier, he had been powerfully muscled with an intimidating appearance. He was now fifty-five years old and running a little to lard, but he still commanded a lot of respect, and he was fearless as well as fully experienced at his trade.

He was pouring coffee into a tin cup at the

wood-stove when Jake Beam entered the dingy little office, and turned slowly without nodding or speaking, then finished drawing off the coffee and went massively to his desk and sat down as he said, 'Good morning . . . Coffee's hot if you'd like a cup.'

Mister Beam ignored the coffee pot. 'Charley Whitson was coming out of the horse-barn yesterday in the late afternoon, and someone shot him.'

The township marshal leaned forward gazing at Mister Beam. 'Killed him?'

'Dead as a rock . . . Bushwhacked him right before my eyes. I was standing by the hitchrack.'

'Did you find the gunman?'

'No. The boys went after him. He came toward town, but they lost his tracks near here; there were too many other tracks.'

Tom Hedrich continued to regard the cowman through an interval of silence, then he said, 'Why?'

'I got no idea, Marshal. None at all. We talked about that last night. There just don't seem to be any reason—except that of course there was one . . . He wasn't crazy, Marshal. He waited somewhere east of the yard. We haven't found the place yet, but we will. And he let Charley get half way between me and the barn— a good target—then killed him. Cold-blooded murder—planned just exactly the way it

13

happened.'

Marshal Hedrich sat like a big stone carving. He had known Charley as well as he had known any of the rangemen in his territory, and had liked him. He had in fact known Charley better than he had known Mister Beam, and, privately, he had liked him a lot more.

Hedrich picked up the coffee cup and drank from it. When he put it aside he said, 'Toward town?'

'Yes. And his horse was wearing new shoes.'

Hedrich brightened slightly. 'All right. If his horse was shod here in town they'll remember him. That's where I'll start. What else?'

Jake Beam went to a chair and sat down, silent for a long moment. 'I don't know ... I'll tell you something I discovered by pure accident six, eight years ago ... But I don't see how it would have anything to do with what happened. And I never talked to Charley about it. It was his business ... I never talked to anyone about it until right now ... One time during marking season I was on a ridge northwest of the home place, just sitting on my horse up there getting warm and watching them bring in cattle. Charley was maybe a half-mile northward around the same hill I was sitting on. There was two In'ians. One was a woman. Her and Charley was arguing.'

'How do you know that; could you hear them?'

14

'Marshal, Charley and I worked a long time together. The only time he used his hands was when he was mad or upset about something. He was using them with that In'ian woman. They was arguing.'

'What was the other In'ian doing?'

'Settin on his horse maybe five yards away looking on and not making a sound. He had a little kid behind him on his horse, but I didn't see the little kid until the woman called the buck over closer and pointed to him as she talked to Charley ... Charley stopped waving his arms and sat there like he didn't know what to say or do ... When the woman finished, Charley fished in his pants pocket and handed her a wad of greenbacks. We'd had payday two days earlier. She took the money, and the two of them—with the little kid—turned and rode toward the mountains.'

Marshal Hedrich thought about that for a long time. 'What did you make of it, Mister Beam?'

'The same thing you'd have made of it, Marshal.'

'And what would that be?'

Mister Beam squirmed a little in the chair. 'She likely was telling Charley it was his kid. And he gave her money.'

Hedrich gazed down at his two large hands atop the old desk. 'You figure he wouldn't have done that if he didn't think it was his kid.'

15

'Yes ... But hell, that was maybe eight years ago. If she'd wanted to shoot Charley, it's not reasonable to expect that she'd wait so damned long, is it?'

Marshal Hedrich avoided an answer because he had first-hand knowledge of people waiting even longer to get revenge. He took his tin cup back to the stove and refilled it. He was much less happy about this episode than he had been about the new horseshoes, for a very good reason. Finding an Indian—of either sex—was impossible unless the Indian did not care whether he—or she—was found. Especially in the northward mountains which ran for five hundred miles in an east-west sprawl.

He went back to his chair. 'What did she look like, Mister Beam?'

'I wasn't that close, Marshal. Only I'd judge she was a young woman, from the way she moved and all. The man with her was a lot older, skinny and sort of stooped ... Marshal, I'm telling you this in confidence. You understand?'

'Yes, I understand ... except that whatever Charley did maybe ten years or more ago isn't goin' to matter to Charley now, is it?'

'All the same ...'

'All right ... Anything else he might have done that'd make someone want to shoot him?'

'Nothing. I thought about that over and over. Since he's worked for Pine Cone he's never been

16

in any serious trouble. Not that I know of anyway, and I'd have known most likely if he had.'

Tom Hedrich nodded a little absently. 'If you find where the bushwhacker hid, don't touch anything. I'll be out in a day or two. Meanwhile I'll keep my fingers crossed that the town blacksmith will remember the new shoes and the feller who had them tacked on. What colour horse was he riding?'

Jake Beam did not know. 'The cook saw someone riding away fast, but he was too far off for the cook to be able to make out anything about him or his horse.'

The silence ran on for a while, then Jake Beam arose. 'Five hundred dollars reward, Marshal.'

Hedrich nodded and arose as his visitor departed. He stood at a barred little front-wall recessed window watching the cowman cross to the general store, which also had the postal franchise, and emerge moments later with the ranch mail.

Mister Beam, he told himself, was one of those men it was possible to respect without liking. Then Hedrich went down to the blacksmith's shop, and was intercepted on the way by a black-headed man whose brown eyes beneath the droop of an old hat were habitually narrowed, with squint wrinkles at their outer edges. The marshal said, 'You want to take a long ride on a long chance, Sam? Someone killed Mister Beam's rangeboss yesterday ... That means there is a foreman's job open.'

The dark-eyed man had a stocky build. He could never have been classified in cow country as anything other than a rangeman. He thinly smiled at the lawman. 'Obliged, Tom. It's nice riding weather.' He lightly slapped the marshal on the shoulder and walked across the wide roadway in the direction of the liverybarn.

Hedrich continued down to the smithy where one of the quickest-tempered and most disagreeable people in Rochester conducted a blacksmithing and wagon works. His name was Frank English and he wore glasses which he was forever having to remove to clean; there were few occupations under the sun where wearing eye-glasses was more of a handicap. If it wasn't forge-dust, or greasy fingers, it was raw sweat which made looking through eye-glasses like looking through the bottom of a dirty fish bowl.

Maybe that was what had made Frank English such a disagreeable individual. He was wiping his glasses on a blue handkerchief when Marshal Hedrich walked in, and eyed the big lawman with no great fondness as he hooked the glasses back into place.

Hedrich told English about the Pine Cone foreman's murder. English spat amber to one side and showed neither pity nor genuine interest until Hedrich asked about new shoes,

18

then Frank said, 'Tom; gawddammit, we've shod maybe fifteen horses in the past week. How the hell would you expect me to remember all those people? And my helper's shod some I didn't even see.'

'Try,' said the big man, looking steadily at the blacksmith, with whom he'd had run-ins before.

'You got anything else to go on?'

'No. You remember Charley.'

'Yes, I remember him ... What colour horse?'

'I don't know.'

English's lean, rugged face began to redden. 'All right; I'll find my magic wand and ...'

'Frank, let me tell you something. This hasn't started out to be a very good day for me.'

They stood facing one another. A powerfully muscled younger man passed through, saw them, and went to the water bucket to reach for the dipper as he continued to watch them from the corner of his eye. He had worked at the smithy for a year now and had taken his share of abuse from Frank English, and although he had been looking for other employment around Rochester, thus far he had found nothing, so he was bleakly hanging on to his job. But he did not know how much longer he would be able to.

He was hoping his employer would say the wrong thing and get knocked flat, but instead Frank suddenly whirled on his heels and went slamming in the direction of his soot-grimed

19

little cubbyhole of an office. He said, 'Come along, Tom. I got a record book. We'll go over that.'

CHAPTER THREE

ONE MAN'S RESOLVE

They buried Charley inside the little wrought-iron fence which encircled the Pine Cone cemetery. There were six other graves out there, all of rangemen except for the one set a little apart beneath a huge old cottonwood tree. That was the burial site of Jake Beam's Ute woman.

Harold Tatum, sweating like a boar hog and turned out in his town-coat, which was getting a little green from age, read from a Bible. Abel and Cotton and Jake Beam stood bare-headed, and only raised their eyes when movement back in the direction of the yard caught their attention.

Morales had returned. Before the others got back with the wagon, Morales had cared for his animal and was at the cookhouse table eating with both hands. He had neither shaved nor washed since before leaving. His clothing was stained, and when the others trooped in he looked at their attire, guessed where they had been, what they had done, and reached for a cup of coffee as they came over to the opposite side of the table to look at him. All but Harold, who got rid of his town-coat, shed his old boots for a pair of slippers and returned from his room out back to start a meal.

Morales pushed the empty cup away and looked straight at Jake Beam. 'I didn't find him,' he said, and ate a little more before speaking again. 'But he was riding a sorrel horse with a long stride—maybe sixteen hands tall. And young, because the horse—he loped loose and easy.'

Mister Beam thumbed back his hat as he sat down and leaned on the table. 'Where did he go?'

'Well; he went to Rochester.'

'Morales, we guessed that much.'

The black eyes lingered on Beam. 'But he stopped before he got there, on the outskirts.'

Abel frowned. 'You sure? There was a hell of a lot of tracks down there, Juan.'

'I'm sure, Abel. When we went after him the light was getting bad. Me, I had good light and lots of time. He stopped in some trees and I think he stood in there with his carbine. There was the imprint of a steel butt-plate. He was waiting. It's a damned good thing we wasn't on his heels—him in the trees and us chargin' up there like a bunch of In'ians.'

Morales wiped his mouth with a soiled sleeve and groped in a pocket to bring forth two items.

One was a brass carbine casing, the other item was some clotted dirt with tiny pebbles and rotting tree leaves embedded in it. They all knew what the casing was, but the lump of dirt had them scowling.

Morales took his time. 'He didn't eject the casing after shooting Charley. I guess he didn't want anyone to find it where he was hiding when he fired. He ejected it over in them trees. He'd have to anyway, if anyone had been chasing him.'

Cotton pointed. 'What's that?'

Morales arose, went after a cup and poured some of the cook's hot water into it, then he lowered the clot of dirt, and as they all watched, the water turned blood red. Morales sat down again, and waited.

Jake Beam raised narrowed eyes. 'Nobody shot at him, Morales.'

The cowboy shrugged. 'It is blood, Mister Beam.'

Cotton sat down and peered into the cup. 'Maybe he was shot before . . . Hey, maybe him and Charley met somewhere.'

Jake Beam snorted. 'Where? You was all together yesterday bringing in the horses. If there'd been a fight . . .'

Morales interrupted. 'No, I don't think so. I think that is spit.'

The cook came over scowling darkly. 'Spit? Damn it, why didn't you use an empty tin can,

22

Juan?'

Abel leaned back a little. 'A lunger.'

They all thought that over. Jake Beam finally arose, 'A lunger riding a sorrel horse with new shoes on. There is a little daylight left, maybe we can find where he hid when he fired.'

Cotton was on his feet looking at the tophand when he said, 'We already found it, Mister Beam. While you was in town and we had nothing else to do.'

Mister Beam strode to the door. 'Show me.'

Late afternoon was settling by the time they got out there. Morales was the best sign-reader among them, but they had all tracked their share of horses and cattle, and had grown up understanding their environment and the impressions men and animals and Mother Nature made upon it.

The bushwhacking site was a depression lying not very far from the yard in a northeasterly direction. Jake Beam's father, who was a good man at signs, had often said that if someone dug there, they'd bring in a good water-well. No one had ever done it because there was a sump-spring behind the main-house which had been easier to develop.

Morales swung off and pointed. 'That's where he was lying. Maybe two, three hours.' He raised his arm and pointed due northward toward a distant spit of trees, perhaps a half-mile away. 'You go up there, Cotton?'

The light-haired cowboy nodded. 'Yeah. There's horse tracks and droppings in among the trees.'

Morales turned toward his employer, waiting. Mister Beam did not dismount. He sat his saddle with both hands resting lightly on the horn, looking at the faint impression where a prone body had pressed the grass flat, then he raised his eyes in the direction of the trees and wagged his head. 'One of us should have seen him runnin' up there for his horse.'

Perhaps one of them should have, but they hadn't. It was not every day they saw a friend shot down; they had been concerned for Charley.

Abel lifted his hat to scratch as he said, 'That was risky. For all he knew we might have still had the horses saddled in the barn.'

Jake Beam blew out a ragged long breath and turned to lead the way back, and when they were dismounting in front of the horse barn, he leaned on the rack as he spoke.

'We're going to get this son of a bitch. I'm goin' back to town. You fellers settle in. If I see a light when I get back, I'll come over to the bunkhouse.'

They stood mutely watching Mister Beam unloop his reins and swing back across leather, and after he was out of the yard Abel Carnes was leading his horse inside to be unsaddled when he said, 'I wouldn't want to be in that

24

bushwhacker's boots.'

It was still warm, but dark, by the time Jake Beam reached Rochester. The town was lighted, and although the general store was locked up for the night, as were other commercial establishments, the pool hall, saloon, liverybarn and one or two other places were still open for business.

Beam left his horse with the liveryman and went in search of the township marshal. He found him at the cafe lingering over supper, and Hedrich looked surprised when Mister Beam dropped down beside him at the counter, and waved the cafeman away before starting to speak.

'We found where he was lying when he fired, and Morales, my *vaquero*, went down his backtrail and came back saying the man was riding a sixteen-hands-high sorrel horse.'

Marshal Hedrich pushed his plate away and leaned on the counter. He knew Juan Morales. 'What else did he find?'

'Spit. He found where the feller waited in some trees to see if anyone was shagging him, and he spat. It was bloody spit ... I figure, unless he had a wound, that he was a lunger.'

Tom Hedrich regarded the hard-jawed older man. 'Sorrel horse, sixteen hands tall. English ought to remember that. A lunger ... You did right well, Mister Beam. I'll talk to Doc Lord an' find out if he's treated anyone with

25

tuberculosis lately.'

Jake Beam said, 'When? When will you see the doctor and Frank English?'

'Well; in the morning.'

Mister Beam's unrelenting gunmetal eyes hardened toward the marshal. 'If you're too busy to do it right now, I'll do it.' He arose.

Hedrich's colour mounted. He had a rebuke on the tip of his tongue, but experience told him he had better not say it, so he also arose, flung down some coins and followed Jake Beam out in the moonless, warm night.

'Frank will throw a tantrum,' he told the cowman, as they started toward a southward intersecting roadway.

Mister Beam was not intimidated. 'He can do whatever he wants to do. Lettin' grass grow under a man's feet don't accomplish anything.'

Tom Hedrich was correct. When the blacksmith opened his front door and saw who was standing under the overhang on his porch, he yanked the napkin loose which had been tucked inside his collar and without a greeting of any kind, said, 'Is there some damned reason why business can't be conducted during business hours?'

Mister Beam answered bleakly. 'A damned good reason. I want the son of a bitch who shot my rangeboss, and the time of day don't have anything to do with it.'

English stepped out and closed the door at his

back. He had been eating supper. Being interrupted at a meal was certain to spark his disagreeableness. He looked at Jake Beam and had both fists clenched at his sides when he spoke. 'Tom and I already went over my shoeing book at the shop. Neither me nor my helper can help you a damned bit, Mister Beam. We shod over fifteen horses this past...'

'You just listen,' snarled Jake Beam, not yielding an inch. 'It was a sorrel horse, sixteen hands tall, and fairly young.'

English turned his glare upon the lawman. 'All you told me...'

'Frank, until half an hour ago I didn't know any more than I told you. Mister Beam just come into town with this new information.'

English remained stiff and defiant, but now he was silent for a long time, and while his visitors watched him and waited, he unclenched his fists and relaxed slightly. Then he ignored Mister Beam and turned to face Marshal Hedrich as he spoke. 'All right. You remember in the book I showed you the entry for a horse that needed a slight correction for pigeon-toes?'

Hedrich remembered. 'Yes. You shod him last Monday.'

'He was sorrel, and he was tall. I remember him because he was so tall. And while I didn't mouth him, I can tell you he wasn't no more'n six years old.'

Jake Beam said, 'What did his rider look

like?'

But Frank English was through talking to Mister Beam. He replied by still regarding the marshal, and as though Hedrich had asked the question. 'Nondescript, skinny feller, about forty maybe ... I don't recollect that he was even carrying a belt-gun, and there sure as hell was no saddleboot ... Brown hair—needed cutting—otherwise he looked like a hundred other fellers.'

Jake Beam had another question. 'What did he talk about; where was he from and all?'

Frank English had his back to Mister Beam. His answer again was offered to Marshal Hedrich. 'He didn't talk much. Told me he wanted a new set all around, and asked where the cafe was, which made me know he was a stranger in town, and that he must have rode in from the south, because if he had come down from the north to my shop, he would have rode past the cafe and seen it ... That's all he said. When he came back for the horse couple hours later, he paid, nodded and led the horse out. Didn't say a single word. Not even thank you. What the hell do people think a blacksmith is, some kind of machine that you don't have to treat civil?'

Jake Beam cleared his throat and reached in a pocket. The blacksmith saw the pressed-flat packet of greenbacks and with a sizzling curse, wrenched open the door, stepped through and

28

slammed it after himself so hard the porch floor reverberated.

Mister Beam stood with the money in his hand looking steadily at the door, and Tom Hedrich said, 'Come along. I figure the doctor will still be up.' As he walked back toward the main part of town, Hedrich decided that if those two mean-tempered men ever met with no one around to step between them, one of them would not walk away. He wondered why it had never happened before; both of them had been in the Portales country most of their lives. Maybe it had happened, but without weapons.

When Mister Beam caught up, and they were back at the intersection, he said, 'We're getting somewhere, Marshal,' and led off at a brisk pace in the direction of the doctor's lighted cottage, which was upon the west side of the main road at the upper end of town.

Hedrich said nothing, he just lengthened his stride to keep up, and he told himself that maybe the reason those two cranky bastards had never tangled was because once Mister Beam got what he had come for, he turned his back and walked away. English wouldn't have; he'd have stood there talking mean until the cows came home. Maybe that was the difference between a successful, big cow rancher, and a town blacksmith whose hands always smelled foul from handling the feet of horses with thrush.

They were nearing the little white picket gate

in the doctor's front fence when Mister Beam turned and said, 'Have you told folks about that five-hundred-dollar reward?'

Hedrich looked down. 'Mister Beam, you only told me about it this morning.'

'Marshal . . . Oh hell, forget it. A man's born the way he becomes and all the lecturing in the world won't change a lazy one who figures he's got all day to do things.'

Mister Beam passed through the gate, went to the porch and rattled the door with a work-scarred set of big knuckles. Tom Hedrich came up more slowly, his face set in an expression which suggested he might be nearing the end of his tether.

CHAPTER FOUR

RIDDLES

Doctor Henry Lord was a short, paunchy individual with clear blue eyes, a goatee which made his round, plump face look a little less like a pink melon, and an air of calm confidence. He had been an army surgeon before arriving in the Portales country some twelve years earlier. He had two grown sons who lived somewhere back east, and a wife built along the same lines, sturdy, not very tall, and with an expression of calm, maybe fatalistic, acceptance.

When he admitted his visitors and nodded a greeting, Mister Beam scarcely allowed the doctor time enough to get the door closed before he asked if Doctor Lord had any knowledge of someone suffering from tuberculosis, and the doctor did not reply until he had led his guests into a sparkling clean but completely unadorned little waiting room, and motioned them towards chairs. In his own domain, no one barged in, took command, and fired questions at him. Seated behind a little flat table Doctor Lord gazed dispassionately from Mister Beam to Marshal Hedrich, and ignored Jake Beam's questions as he quietly said, 'There are very few medical men, that I know of, who discuss their patients with outsiders.'

Tom Hedrich was embarrassed. He told the entire story in a calm and measured tone, beginning with the killing of Charley Whitson, and ending up with what he and Mister Beam had just learned from the blacksmith. When he finished speaking the round, soft body of Doctor Lord loosened where he sat and his clear gaze came around to Jake Beam, whom he had known for about eight years. 'A murderer is different,' he announced, then allowed a moment to pass before speaking again. He knew how to retrieve the initiative; that was one of the artifices of his trade. 'As a matter of fact, Mister Beam, I have about eleven tubercular patients in

31

the countryside.'

'Tall, skinny man,' stated Mister Beam. 'About forty. Don't seem to talk much. A stranger, Doctor Lord.'

Again, the medical practitioner allowed moments to pass. He was setting Jake Beam straight about personal conduct. 'I have several tall, thin tubercular patients, Mister Beam, but I've known every one of them for a long time. The only new tubercular patient I've had in months was a woman in her late twenties. All I know about her, aside from the extent of her disease, is that her name is Margerie . . . just a moment.' Henry Lord delved in the top drawer of his little white table, placed a book atop it, and slowly went through the pages. 'Here it is. Age twenty-six . . . I thought she might be a little older . . . Margerie Whitson Baker.'

Jake Beam sat perfectly still staring at Doctor Lord, who went on speaking. Marshal Tom Hedrich was also motionless on his chair, staring.

'Her husband is Ronald Baker. According to this entry he is in the freighting business.' Doctor Lord closed the little book and raised his eyes. 'That is the only stranger I've treated for . . . What is the matter with you two?'

Jake Beam ignored the question. Marshal Hedrich said, 'Henry, that's the name of Mister Beam's foreman who got killed from ambush. Whitson.'

32

Doctor Lord remained calm, but for a while he had nothing to say. When he finally returned the little book to its drawer and closed it, he leaned back in the chair eyeing Jake Beam. 'I don't think it's that common a name, Mister Beam.'

The cowman gently inclined his head. 'Charley was the only person I ever knew with that name, Doctor.'

'Well, Mister Beam, I can tell you one thing: This woman did not ride a horse out where your buildings are, shoot someone, then ride back to Rochester. She has advanced tuberculosis. I told her husband the only thing I knew of which might at least relieve her suffering, would be to take her down to the south desert country in either New Mexico or Arizona where the air is hot and dry. Otherwise, I doubted that she would see next Christmas ... Well, gentlemen ... ?'

Marshal Hedrich was on his feet when he said, 'Are they stayin' around town, Henry?'

Doctor Lord also arose. 'I don't know, Tom. I only know she was here twice. I did what I could for her. There was no point in asking her to come back, so I didn't make another appointment for her.'

Jake Beam went all the way through to the roadside door and had his hand on the latch before he spoke again. 'Is her husband a tall, skinny feller, maybe forty?'

Doctor Lord regarded Mister Beam steadily for a moment before answering. He knew human nature; he also knew Jake Beam, mostly from hearsay but it had been undeviating in its implication. He knew exactly what a man like Mister Beam had in mind concerning the killing of one of his riders.

Doctor Lord went out onto his front porch with them and admired the moonless but star-riddled warm night sky. 'Mister Beam, her husband isn't forty. I'd say he was closer to thirty or maybe a year or two into his thirties ... Yes, he is rather tall. Not as tall as Tom here, but a tad over average height.'

'And skinny?'

'... He is a spare-built man, yes, but I'd like to make a suggestion, Mister Beam. Before you run them down and make a hangrope, you find out all you can about them.'

Jake was settling his hat on his head when he said, 'What do I owe you? Not for your damned advice, but for your time.'

Doctor Lord tilted an expression of resignation in Tom Hedrich's direction, went back inside his house without speaking, and gently closed the door.

The marshal plunged big fists deep into trouser pockets and gazed in the direction of the saloon lights. Beside him, Jake Beam closed and latched the little picket gate, and said, 'I don't understand this, Marshal ... Morales said a man stood in the trees watching his back trail. Doctor Lord said the woman was a lunger, not the man. But if she was out there, maybe waiting for him to come back after killing Charley, why didn't Morales see the sign of two people among the trees?'

Marshal Hedrich was thinking differently. 'Did Charley maybe have a wife down his backtrail somewhere? Maybe a woman sick with the lung fever? Mister Beam, how old was Charley?'

That was a question which had never arisen before, nor did the age of his rangemen concern Mister Beam. Nor did he think about it, not in them and not in himself. He said, 'I don't know, Marshal. You want a guess? I'd say Charley was maybe forty, maybe forty-five. But I'm no good at guessing people's ages. He could have been older for all I know . . . Or younger.'

'. . . A daughter, Mister Beam?'

For a while the cowman leaned on the gate saying nothing, then he shoved upright and started away. 'Good night, Marshal. I'm going home. If you want to come out and look at that place where the bushwhacker lay, I'll be there,' then he paused and looked around. 'If you're of a mind to see if they stayed at the roominghouse . . .'

Marshal Hedrich nodded unenthusiastically and as he watched Mister Beam fade in the darkness, he grunted. No one who had

35

deliberately committed murder and who knew he had left tracks which could be followed would come back to town and bed down at the roominghouse. Not even a damned fool would do that.

The warmth was leaving as the high rash of stars brightened, and throughout Rochester the lights had been going out for a couple of hours. It was not especially late, but in country where people of habit ordinarily retired between eight and nine o'clock, it was past bedtime.

For Mister Beam, the ride back was long, and before he reached the yard, also cold. He missed feeling any discomfort for the first hour or so, because he was beginning to feel as though he had opened someone's can of worms. The things he now knew troubled him, and they did not make a lot of sense, either.

The bunkhouse was dark when he entered the yard from the east. He was relieved because he did not know what, exactly, conclusion to draw, which meant he would have been unable to explain things to the satisfaction of Cotton and Abel.

He looped his reins out front, hauled the saddle inside to the pole, flung it across and returned to lead his horse around back by the bridle reins. Except for an owl mournfully calling at regular intervals off to the west somewhere, there was not a sound until Jake Beam opened the pole gate, and where it was grounded on a flat stone, it made an abrasive sound. He slipped the bridle, slapped the horse lightly on the rump and turned away after latching the gate, without seeing the horse go down in front and roll over and back, twice. Stockmen had a saying that for each time a horse could roll completely over and back, he was worth a hundred dollars. Mister Beam's animal was worth four hundred, and his owner did not even know it.

Jake Beam did not retire. He lit a lamp in the parlour of the main-house, hung his hat from an antler-rack, rubbed his bristly jaw and got a bottle and glass from a glass-fronted cupboard, then sat down to unbuckle his spurs and toss them aside. He sipped Old Crow, propped his feet atop a little table, and thought about his dead foreman.

There was an old cowboy buried out yonder who had been grizzled and grey as a badger when Jake had been young. He had hired on with Jake's father and had died in his sleep eleven years later, which was probably a blessing because his hands were getting too stiff and knotty to do much. He had once told Jake that you never really knew folks; you thought you did, because they always combed their hair the same way and used the same words when they cussed, but you never did; every man had his inner self which only he and maybe one or two other folks knew about.

Jake sipped and thought of times when he and Charley Whitson had worked side by side. They had made a good team and Charley was a loyal Pine Cone rider, but during all those years neither of them had mentioned personal things to the other.

So someone had come along and for some damned reason had killed Charley with one shot from ambush.

And who was that woman named Whitson Baker? Jake finished his whiskey and hauled his carcass off to bed. He was tired only from the neck down, but the whiskey took care of that. He slept like a log and only awakened when he heard men talking out in the yard.

The sun was fully up. Jake Beam rolled out and hurried to get out there. The last time he had slept past sunrise had been when he'd had a bout of fever six or seven years earlier.

The men were down in the barn. He let them wait while he went to the cookshack and under old Harold's curious gaze, got fed. Just before leaving the cookhouse he said, 'When you saw someone ridin' pell-mell eastward, Harold ... did you see anything before that?'

The *cocinero* shook his head. Abel had asked him the same thing. 'No. I was makin' for the front porch when I heard the gunshot, Mister Beam. If that feller run for his horse amongst the trees, I likely wouldn't have seen him anyway since the building cut me off from a

38

sighting in that direction ... Mind me askin'
what come of your ride into town last night?'

Jake Beam did not mind, particularly, he just
did not want to stand in the cookshack doorway
gabbling, so he said, 'We'll talk about it tonight
at supper,' and went on down to the barn.

There was a stranger in the runway with Abel
and Cotton, which surprised Jake Beam. The
man was compactly built with black hair and
eyes. He was probably light bronze in colour
even when he had not been out in the sun, but
now he was an even darker shade of bronze. He
looked to be in his middle or late thirties, and
when he faced around and saw Mister Beam stop
stone-still in the doorway staring, he smiled and
said, 'My name is Sam Bolt ... If you're hiring,
Mister Beam, I'm willing.'

Cotton and Abel were watching both men,
obviously interested. Mister Beam walked
closer. 'Where is your horse, Mister Bolt?'

'Tied to the corral out back. I got my
gatherings.'

Mister Beam studied the calm, bronze face.
He knew a rangeman when he saw one and Sam
Bolt was one. But Mister Beam was curious.
'You just rode up, on your own, or did someone
tell you we might be short-handed?'

Sam Bolt wore an old ivory-stocked Colt in a
brush-scratched holster. His boots were worn,
his trousers and shirt were faded. He had roping
gloves of split cowhide shoved carelessly under

his shellbelt, and his silver-mounted spurs had cut down Chihuahua rowels. If Sam Bolt was not tophand or rangeboss material, then he was about the best imitation of them Mister Beam had ever seen.

'I just sort of rode in,' he told Mister Beam, then hung fire before adding a little more. 'Over in Rochester I heard a couple of your riders quit.'

'What else did you hear, Mister Bolt?'

The black eyes were stone-steady. 'That your rangeboss got shot here in your yard by a bushwhacker. That's all.'

Jake Beam had finished his appraisal. His face relaxed slightly. 'We got a lot of work to do, Mister Bolt, and we'll still be short-handed, which means until we can pick up another man or two, you're likely to have to work your butt off.'

Sam Bolt smiled slowly. 'I don't know any other way to work, Mister Beam.'

'One more question, Mister Bolt: I don't know who killed my foreman. For all I know there's a son of a bitch out yonder who just wants to kill Pine Cone riders.'

Bolt shrugged very faintly. 'I thought about that.'

'You still want to hire on?'

'Yes sir.'

'Sam is it?'

'Yes sir, Sam Bolt.'

40

'Go dump your gatherings in the bunkhouse, Sam, then come back and turn your horse out. If you haven't eaten this morning, Harold will tank you up at the cookshack.'

After the new man had walked out back to untie his bedroll and possible-bag and head for the bunkhouse, Mister Beam went to lean on the saddle pole as he said, 'He just came in, Abel?'

'Yeah. We was goin' out to catch our horses for the day, and there he was . . . I think you did a good lick when you hired him.'

'You know him, ever see him before?'

'No, but he's a cowman or I never saw one, Mister Beam . . . And like you said, we're still short a man or two.'

Cotton waited until there was a strung-out interval of silence, then said, 'What come of your ride into town last night?'

Jake Beam pushed up off the saddle-pole. 'We'll talk about it as we ride out and see if we can get a handle on making that gather we was supposed to work on last week . . . and we'll have a chance to watch Sam Bolt too.'

CHAPTER FIVE

SAM BOLT

Perhaps because it was a little later than it should have been for men on their way to work cattle, they got only slightly beyond the spit of trees where the bushwhacker had tied his horse, and Jake Beam was listening to the explanation of Juan Morales about having found no sign of a second person down yonder near Rochester where that man had stood in the trees with his carbine, when Cotton raised a gloved hand and said, 'Rider.'

It was Marshal Hedrich on a flashy sorrel with a flaxen mane and tail. Mister Beam watched Hedrich approach, and finally said, 'You boys go ahead and get started. I'll be along when I can ... Abel; you know what to do.'

The rangemen eased over into a lope. Jake Beam waited alone until Tom Hedrich arrived, then he nodded and said, 'You eaten? It's a short ride back to the yard if you haven't.'

The lawman had eaten before leaving town. He dismounted and turned to watch the Pine Cone men for a moment. Then he said, 'They didn't stay at the roominghouse,' and faced back around. 'I almost didn't ride out this morning, and I got to get straight back. I think if that woman's as sick as Henry Lord said she was, and if they're travelling on horseback or maybe in a wagon, I can make up a posse and scatter 'em out over the territory and maybe find them ... What did Morales say?'

'That there was no other foot-tracks where the feller waited among the trees to see if my riders would find him.'

'Well ... Either Henry was wrong and the man's also a lunger, or she was there maybe waiting for him to get back after the killing, and didn't leave any tracks.'

'How do you do that, Marshal?'

'I don't know, Mister Beam, but standing here isn't going to help me find out, is it?'

'Come along. I'll show you where he had his horse hid, and where he was lyin' when he shot Charley.'

They rode back to the trees in silence. Hedrich stepped down and quartered the area reading as much sign as he could, then they rode closer to the yard and Jake Beam showed him where the bushwhacker had been lying. But the grass was not as pressed down as it had been, and otherwise there was nothing much to be seen.

As the lawman was swinging up again Jake Beam fished in a vest pocket and held out the brass casing. 'Morales found it over near town where he stood in the trees. Maybe you got use for it, I don't.'

Marshal Hedrich studied the casing on the palm of his hand. 'There is one other thing, Mister Beam. I felt obliged to tell you what I think about those folks moving through, and I expect you got plenty of work to do here on the ranch . . .'

Mister Beam met the larger and younger man's gaze. 'Go on.'

'Leave this up to me, Mister Beam. Me an' a posse. I understand how you feel and all, but if they can be overtaken, I'll do it. And like I said, you most likely got plenty to keep you busy on the ranch.'

Old Jake stonily regarded the lawman for a while before speaking again, and then he was short. 'I'm glad you rode out, Marshal, and it's been nice talking to you.' He then spun his horse and went loping in the direction his riders had taken.

Marshal Hedrich watched for a moment then also rode away, but in a different direction, toward town, and he was not as irritated as Mister Beam had been, so he did not take it out on his horse. In fact he did not lope the big flashy sorrel until he had walked him a mile.

To make the kind of gather Pine Cone was embarking upon it was necessary to split up the crew so that as much as a mile, or even two miles, separated the men. Abel had begun peeling them off as soon as the entire crew was about four miles out. He detailed Cotton Buford

and Sam Bolt to scour out the foothills from east
to west, riding a mile or two apart, and anything
they found they were to push out to open
country where they could be seen.

As soon as Sam and Cotton passed around the
first little rough foothills they were lost to sight
to anyone coming up from the south, which was
why Mister Beam did not see them, and kept
riding on an easterly angle, following the tracks
of his other two riders, Abel Carnes and Juan
Morales.

Nor did they see Mister Beam. The foothills
were not very deep, but they skirted all along
the lower front of the higher mountains and
although there were stands of pines, they were
infrequent and where the rotting stumps stood
now to show why they were infrequent,
underbrush had taken over. Pine Cone had been
getting its winter wood in these foothills for a
great many years. There were faint wagon ruts
completely overgrown, and there were much
fresher ruts. Also, there were a number of little
creeks and springs through the entire chain of
shallow, low hills. It was, Sam Bolt observed
before he and Cotton Buford split up, ideal
country for calving cows.

Cotton had been brushing out these same
foothills since his first season at Pine Cone and
loped steadily farther westward to scour out the
habitual bedding and calving grounds. Sam
Bolt, who did not know these foothills, sought

cattle by sign, and also by scent. He found his first little bunch serenely at rest in tree-shade beside a flowing spring, and because he arrived behind them atop a low landswell, and sat motionless, they did not notice him. But when he started down in their direction they sprang up, all but one heifer, and with tails over their backs like scorpions, fled westward. The down-critter threshed and flung her head, but did not stand up.

Sam rode closer and watched for a moment, then swung off, shed his gloves, took down his lariat and took a couple of steps closer, teasing to see if the heifer had enough strength left to jump up. If she did, Sam was closer to his horse than she was.

But she didn't arise; she floundered and flung slobbers and rolled bulging eyes at Sam, and shook her horns, but she was dark with sweat all over. She was weak from straining; she had a hung-up calf, which Sam speculated was probably dead by now if she had been in this condition very long. But it still had to come out, or there'd also be a dead heifer. He sighed, walked still closer, waited out an interlude of frantic threshing as the desperate heifer struggled with all her remaining strength to arise. When she fell back, eyes rolling, sweat dropping to the ground in thin trickles, Sam walked around, saw about what he expected, one protruding little pasty-white hoof and foreleg, and paused to roll up his sleeves before going ahead to kneel, plunge his hand and arm in until he found the hung-up leg, which he forced downward and outward, then made his loop and yelled, and the moment the agitated cow strained, Sam set all his weight on the slack. Half the head emerged. Sam eased up, waited, then yelled again, and that time when the weakening heifer strained, Sam got the head out, and the rest of the calf came as easily as a greased pig.

He broke the sack, lifted the wet, steamy head and cleared the nostrils and mouth, then watched for signs of life. They arrived, weak but visible, so Sam dragged the feebly jerking calf around to the heifer's head, took off his rope and started back to the horse. He did not mount up at once, but dried his hands and arms on grass, tied his lariat into place, and shoved back his hat while watching the first-calf heifer licking and nudging and lowing at her first baby.

The heifer could not nudge her baby onto his feet because she was too weak yet herself to stand up, but it was early; before evening she would be up and would have her calf up. After that, if coyotes found the afterbirth, which was what they lived on this time of year, the cow would be able to protect her baby and move him away.

Sam smiled and rolled a smoke. It was a

routine chore, but it always made a man feel good when he could make sure both the cow and calf survived. He lit up and turned to swing back into the saddle.

Thirty feet distant was a tall, lean and unsmiling man with a cocked Colt pointing directly at Sam Bolt. There was no horse in sight. It was as though the tall man had come up out of the earth.

Sam had one hand full of mane-hair, the other hand on his saddlehorn, ready to reach for a stirrup. He stopped stone-still. The astonishment passed in moments. He dropped the cigarette and stamped on it, then looked up again.

'You don't need the gun,' he said quietly.

The tall man wig-wagged his gunbarrel. 'Get away from the horse.'

Sam obeyed, and watched the tall man walk closer. 'Mister, there is a tin of sardines in the off-side saddle pocket, and if you don't need them, I'm likely to because it's a long walk back.'

The tall man turned the animal so that when he swung up into Sam's saddle the horse would be between them. He did not say a word and he cocked the Colt when he toed in, watching Sam without even blinking. When he was astride the Pine Cone horse he said, 'Take that gun of yours by the barrel and fling it as far as you can.'

Sam looked pained, but he slowly and

carefully obeyed. Then the tall man fished in the off-side saddle pocket and tossed down the tin of sardines.

Sam waited; the tall man would ride off now, and probably break over into a dead run so that he would be out of handgun range before Sam Bolt could run out where his ivory-handled Colt had landed in the grass. Instead, the tall man motioned for Sam to go around in front of the horse. He said, 'How long you been on Pine Cone?'

When Sam replied they were facing each other head-on. 'One day. I hired on this morning.'

The tall man squinted a little beneath the down-turning front brim of his hat. 'Are you lying?'

'No sir. I rode out there this morning early, and Mister Beam hired me on, I guess because he was short-handed.' Sam cocked his head slightly. 'If I'd been an old hand would it make a difference?'

The tall man holstered his sixgun and evened up the reins without speaking or looking at Sam. He cast one final look ahead, then turned the horse and hooked him into a lope. He did not make the horse run, and Sam did not run back to retrieve his sixgun for a while. Not until the horsethief had disappeared around a fat little low hill with three pine trees on its crest. Even then, he simply walked back, and after locating his weapon he stood shaking soft earth off it and making certain that it had not been harmed when it had landed. Then, finally, with the gun in its holster, he started walked along the tracks of the tall man.

Sam Bolt did not possess a violent temperament. He was one of those rare men of absolute self-control who knew exactly what to do under most circumstances, and without thought of time or anything else, dispassionately did it, as he was doing now when he started out on foot to get back that Pine Cone horse.

He believed the horsethief had a destination, and was not simply going to head out of the country. He also believed the man had a camp, probably not very distant because wherever he had come from, he had come on foot.

When it was possible to do so, Sam trotted like an Indian. When he had open areas to cross where a watcher up ahead could see him coming, he went far out of his way to seek a sheltered, even though more circuitous way, and with the day advancing, he ascended a hill with flourishing stands of red-barked chaparral atop it, and sat down with the sun at his back to look for movement.

The horsethief was about a mile ahead, riding at a walk. He rode slumped and did not look back during all the time Sam watched him.

Sam was going down the west side of the hill when the horsethief turned up a slot between two brushy hills and was lost to sight.

Sam hunkered on his sidehill waiting for the man to emerge, but he never did. Sam smoked a cigarette and continued to wait, and still the horsethief did not appear, so Sam killed his smoke and went down to flat land and trotted.

CHAPTER SIX

A STOLEN HORSE

The sun was off centre before Sam Bolt reached the vicinity of those little brushy hills, and before he began working his way around them, from the north instead of the south, because if the horsethief was watching, he would expect someone to come from the south, the sun was beginning to gain colour; to turn from faded yellow to rusty, dull copper. At this time of year days were longer, but the sun sank lower in spite of lingering daylight. Sam was in no hurry. His main reason for taking a lot of time to get up closer was because, while he was satisfied the horsethief had a camp around there, perhaps in the little valley between the brushy hills, it did not make much sense for him to still be around there. If Sam had been in his boots he would have stopped only long enough to pile on his bedroll, saddlebags, then keep riding. It both

51

worried and puzzled Sam that the man would be wasting time like this, and that made him very cautious as he got into the thorny underbrush and by using both outstretched arms, began working his way through.

He was on the northeasterly slope, progressing westerly, and the mesquite he had to pass through was both dense and full of sharp little thorns.

He moved slowly in order not to make a sound or to allow the bushes, which were in places higher than his head, to quiver or shake.

And he sweated. There was not a breath of air moving up in here, daylong heat had left a dry-hot residue, and although shadows were appearing, it was still hot.

He finally completed his stalk, got around the lower haunch of the hill and could see into the little grassy slot between his hill and the opposite one, about two hundred yards away.

There was a spring in the shaded narrow little valley. Several large old trees grew close to it. The grass was richer here than any other place he had seen lately, which probably meant the ground was sub-irrigated from the spring, and there was a light spring-wagon down there, shafts on the ground.

Sam sat down, flicked a woodtick off his cheek, and studied the camp near the wagon. There was a stone ring with char inside it, so someone had camped here longer than just overnight. There was a grub box on the lowered tailgate of the spring-wagon, and beyond, upon the far side of the rig, someone had strung a stained square of oilproofed canvas from the wagonside to a tree, making a shelter which would be adequate against the sun, or rain.

Sam's Pine Cone mount was hobbled and peacefully cropping grass near the spring. Sam's saddle had been flung over a wagon-side, his bridle and blanket draped with it.

There was no sign of the horsethief. For that matter there was no sign of life down there at all, except for the Pine Cone horse.

Dusk was on its way, but Sam Bolt was in no hurry. For one thing, he had no carbine and from that distance his sixgun would not be good enough. For another reason, the flourishing underbrush ended at the base of his little hill, and beyond that there was no protection for someone approaching the camp.

Maybe that tall man was not down there. Maybe he had gone off somewhere, to shoot a rabbit for supper or just to look the country over, but if that notion was wrong and he saw Sam approaching. . .

Sam settled down to wait. He had not eaten since very early, back in Rochester, but hunger bothered him much less than the thirst did, and there was a large canteen hanging from the hub of the near-side front wagon wheel.

He had plenty of time to decide on his course

of action, and when he had that straight in his mind he wondered what old Beam and his riders would think about Sam riding out with them on his first day of working for Pine Cone, and not returning.

Dusk was coming when Sam finally stirred. Visibility was still good enough for him to be seen the moment he stepped out of the underbrush, but that tantalising canteen and the fact that he had not seen anyone down there since he had first sighted the wagon-camp encouraged him to start down through the underbrush, some of the time on all fours like a stalking Indian.

The Pine Cone horse raised his head and gazed in Sam's direction, his interest sparked perhaps more by scent than sight. But he went back to picking grass.

By the time Sam was at the edge of the underbrush, he was close enough to hear sounds coming occasionally from the far side of the wagon where that texas had been strung.

Unless the horsethief talked to himself, there was someone else over there. He tried to distinguish words and failed. Finally, he drew his belt-gun, stood upright, stepped out of the brush and with probing eyes walked over to the near side of the spring-wagon, lifted the canteen, unscrewed the cap and hoisted the thing, letting cool water trickle down his shirtfront.

Sweat popped out all over him as he re-capped the canteen and hooked it by the strap over the sideboards again. Now, the Pine Cone horse was watching him from a motionless stance. When he sank to his knees peering through from beneath the wagon, the horse showed candid interest.

A man's back was no more than eight feet away. Sam recognised the shirt, vest and hat. He pushed his Colt ahead and crawled. The man spoke quietly. There was a muted reply, and Sam Bolt cleared the wagonside, pushed up to his knees and cocked the sixgun without saying a word. The man pulled straight up, then whirled. They were face to face at less than three feet.

Sam said, 'Get rid of the gun. . . Be careful.'

The horsethief tossed the gun away. Sam remembered that face very well, it was sun-darkened, with grey, troubled eyes and a faintly twisted, wide mouth. Sam gestured. 'Back away. Don't stand up, just back away.'

When the horsethief obeyed and Sam felt safe enough, he looked to his left. In the shaded gloom of the canvas a very pretty woman with enormous blue eyes and a flushed, flawless face, was lying atop some blankets, her forehead sweat-shiny, with some ringlets of reddish-brown hair plastered to it. There was another of those big canteens at her side, and some rolled-up squares of dark cloth.

Sam looked at the motionless horsethief. The man was tall but not very broad nor heavy. Sam eased down the hammer and leathered his gun, then he gestured for the horsethief to go over by the woman under the texas, and as the man moved to obey, Sam retrieved the handgun, looked briefly at it, punched out all the loads, pocketed them and pitched the weapon over the side into the wagon. Then he too got under the shading canvas and sat down looking at his prisoners.

Not a sound broke the stillness until Sam Bolt had finished his appraisal. Then he said, 'Did you ever steal a horse before, mister?'

The tall man shook his head.

Sam could believe it. 'If you ever do it again, don't stop. Not for a hundred miles, an' even then don't stop for very long ... Where are you folks from?'

'The nation.'

Sam eyed them both. 'Is that a fact? Don't either of you look In'ian.'

'Not everyone in Oklahoma is a full-blood,' the man said.

Sam turned toward the woman. She was breathing slowly and watching Sam from those very large blue eyes. Sam smiled a little. The woman did not look very strong. Nor was she a girl. He thought she might be in her twenties, perhaps in her late twenties and the flush which made her face seem red, had a tinge of some

56

darker, more golden shading to it. As the man had said, in the Indian Nation they were not all full-bloods.

He looked back at the man. 'What is your name?'

'Smith. John Smith.'

Sam nodded slowly. 'Mister, you're as poor a liar as you are a horsethief.' When the tall man remained silent Sam shrugged. Names did not ordinarily make much difference anyway. He regarded them both for a long time before speaking again. 'Why did you steal my horse?'

The man settled into a more comfortable position beside the violet-eyed woman before replying. 'Because our horse died, and we had to have another animal to draw the wagon.'

That was direct enough. 'Did you know there's a town about fifteen miles southeastward, where you could have bought another horse, Mister Smith?'

The tall man seemed poised to reply, but he did not speak.

Sam looked at the camping equipment, then back at the man again. 'Do you know much about horses, Mister Smith? For example, did you know that saddle horses will not commonly take kindly to being harnessed between wagon shafts?'

'There was no choice,' the horsethief said. 'I could have worked him up to doing it.'

Sam nodded. 'Maybe. In a couple of days.

And what do you figure I would have been doing during those couple of days? I'd be back with the man who owns that horse and his riding crew. His name is Mister Beam, and I got a notion he's hung horsethieves before.'

'As I said, I had no choice.'

For the first time the woman spoke. 'What is your name?'

'Sam Bolt, ma'm.'

'Do you ride for the Pine Cone ranch, Mister Bolt?'

'Yes. This is my first day. I got hired on this morning . . . Mind if I ask your name, ma'm?'

Before answering she looked at the tall man. He seemed to want to speak, but as before he looked away instead.

The woman with the very dark, violet eyes said, 'My name is Margerie Baker.'

Sam smiled at her. 'And this gent is Mister Baker.' He allowed them no time to refute this. 'You folks should have walked down to Rochester and bought yourselves another horse—a combination horse, one that will ride and pull.' Sam watched the build-up of shadows beyond the texas. He had a problem and saw only one solution to it. He doubted very much that the Pine Cone horse he had been riding would work between shafts, so loading his horsethief and the woman into the wagon and heading for the yard with them was not going to work.

He could not march them the full distance back on foot, especially the woman, who looked very frail even in poor light. He arose and jerked his head for the man to walk out a ways with him. When they were upon the far side of the wagon Sam said, 'You're still on foot. I'm going to saddle up and ride home. In the morning you better start out before sunrise and hike down to Rochester and get yourself another combination horse ... Mister, you're lucky. Except for gettin' thirsty shagging you, and using up the whole damned day getting the horse back, I guess I haven't been hurt too much ... But you get that horse, get back here, hitch up and get the hell out of the country.'

The tall man's grave gaze lingered on Sam Bolt. 'Are you going for the law?'

Sam shook his head. 'Mister Baker—don't do it again. You're not cut out for horsestealing, and your wife wouldn't like being a widow.'

The tall man blurted it out: 'I can't walk down to Rochester. I can't leave her.'

Sam was reaching for the bridle on the sideboard when he said, 'She'll be safe enough. I doubt if even a coyote comes up through here more than once a year.'

'I still can't.'

Sam draped the bridle from the saddlehorn gazing at the tall man. 'Why not?'

'Because she is dying. I can't leave her alone. I only left her today because I had seen you riding in the foothills and was desperate for a horse.'

'Dying?'

'Tuberculosis. Did you notice those wads of cloth on the blankets?'

Sam had noticed them. They had looked like ... He said, 'Blood?'

'Yes ... Today in the heat she rallied. She usually does when it's hot. But come nightfall no matter how I try to keep her warm and all, she gets worse.'

Sam fished around for the makings and made a smoke, which he lit while gazing at the tall man. 'Mister, where you'd ought to be is far south of here, on the south desert. It's hot night and day most of every year. I've known people down there who had what ails her. They were doing good.'

The tall man nodded as though he would speak, then, as he had done before, he looked away and said nothing.

Sam went after the horse, removed the hobbles and led it back to be saddled. If he hadn't had that to do, he would have had to invent something; he needed a little time to think.

As he slowly rigged out the Pine Cone gelding he was silent, but when he was trailing both reins from his left hand and standing hip-shot gazing at the tall man, he said, 'All right. You keep her warm tonight. Build a fire. Find some

60

of that old dry manzanita; it burns like hell and don't smoke ... I'll be back tomorrow with a horse.'

'I'll get the money.'

'No. You pay me when I fetch it back up here ... I'm going to get fired as sure as we're standing here,' Sam said, and mounted the horse. 'First day on the job and I go all over hell, and when I get back I'll ask for tomorrow off to go to town.' He laughed and reined away, setting the horse into a long lope. Behind him, the tall horsethief cried out something, and gestured wildly for Sam to come back, but he kept right on riding.

The tall man went back around where the woman was and sank down. She said, 'You tried. It's not fair at all, what I'm doing to you.'

He raised his face to her. 'He rode off before I could ask him not to say anything about meeting us to the man he works for ... Margerie...'

She smiled directly at him. Her large violet eyes were very bright. 'Ron ... Come closer. You have done more than anyone else would even try to do ... I pray for us both every night, and I particularly ask that the future is better for you. Come closer ... I love you very much.'

CHAPTER SEVEN

TROUBLE

Cotton Buford was out back and saw the new man return. It was dark, there was a light over at the main-house, and at the bunkhouse where Abel and Morales were idly talking over coffee.

Sam put up his Pine Cone horse and crossed to the cookshack, not very hopeful because it was the custom with cow outfits that if a man missed a meal, he had to wait for the next one. But Harold was not a cranky man and he liked company. He eyed Sam Bolt in his cookhouse doorway and picked up a huge ladle as he said, 'Set down. There's plenty left ... Cotton told Mister Beam he couldn't find you, and they figured you maybe got lost.'

Sam sat eyeing the cook. Nobody believed a rangeman got lost. Sam pushed back his hat. The smell of food was making his stomach writhe. 'I expect Mister Beam was mad,' he said as the *cocinero* brought over his meal, with hot coffee.

Harold considered his reply. 'Not exactly mad. Irritated. But then, Mister Beam gets irritated right easy sometimes. I been here a long time.' Harold smiled. 'Danged few weeks have went past when I didn't see him get irritated about something.'

The door opened and Jake Beam walked in, unsmiling, hatless and freshly shaved. He nodded but did not speak until he was seated upon the opposite side of the big table from Sam, and the cook had placatingly set coffee before him. Then he raised his gunmetal eyes and said, 'What happened to you?'

Sam continued to shovel in food as he answered. 'Found some cows near a sump-spring, choused them down a ways, and there was a hung-up heifer. I pulled the calf.'

'That took all day, Mister Bolt?'

Sam went on eating. 'No sir. I lost the horse and had to track him down and catch him.'

Jake Beam sat staring at his new rider. Men lost horses now and then. He'd lost his share of them over the years. He sighed and could not restrain an impulse to say, 'You didn't look too good, Sam, on your first day.'

Bolt put down his eating tools and raised his head a little. At least he was Sam again and not Mister Bolt, which implied old Beam was not all iron. On the ride back he'd had ample time to turn several things over in his mind. One of them had been the interest the Bakers had shown in the outfit—this craggy old stockman— he worked for. Another was the matter of the ambushed foreman. He calmly said, 'I'd like to ask you a question, Mister Beam ... You got any idea who shot your rangeboss?'

63

Jake Beam sat hunched forward staring steadily across the table, and Harold turned from the stove to also regard the new man.

Mister Beam said, 'Why? What's your interest?'

'Well, I had an odd thing happen to me today, and since then I been wondering about a few things.'

'What happened to you, Sam?'

'Mister Beam—I guess maybe you'll fire me for this, but then I was lookin' for work when I came here: You didn't answer my question.'

Harold fidgeted but Jake Beam did not change expression through a long interval of silence, then he said, 'Yes, I got a notion who shot Charley. That is your answer.'

'I reckon so. You got any kind of a description of the bushwhacker?'

'Tall man, skinny ... You want his name? Ronald Baker.'

Sam pushed his empty plate aside and reached for the mug of coffee. He was beginning to feel human again.

They sat looking at one another after Sam had drained his cup. Mister Beam said, 'That's the odd thing that happened to you, eh? You run across that son of a bitch today ... Where; in the foothills? We'll go up there tomorrow. You can lead the way.'

Sam was fishing for the makings when Harold came over from the stove to refill their cups. He would not have missed this for a pocketful of new money.

Sam lighted up and blew out a gust of bluish smoke. 'And hang him, Mister Beam?'

'What do they do with murderers where you hail from, Sam?'

'Depends on who catches them. The law tries them first, then hangs them. Stockmen just hang them ... Mister Beam, I've seen dead men, and they never seemed to care about anything; just the living ones do.'

Jake Beam eased back off the table. He was having a little trouble following the reasoning of his new rider. Right at this moment his temper was also simmering. He was satisfied that Bolt had found Charley Whitson's killer. He was also satisfied he and the crew could find the killer— provided he had not left the country since this afternoon—without Sam Bolt's help. What bothered him was the possibility that Sam Bolt might be troublesome over a range hanging and a hidden grave. Tom Hedrich would explode if he learned that Pine Cone had caught and lynched Charley Whitson's killer, and while neither Carnes, Buford nor Morales would ever open their mouths after leaning on the hang-rope, this coppery-faced man across from him might.

He leaned down on the table again. 'Sam, any place you ever been, they hang bushwhackers. One way or another the sons of bitches get hanged—or shot. You agree?'

Bolt agreed. 'Yes. The trouble is, Mister Beam, sometimes it's been done before, not after, a man's had his say.'

'Murder is murder, Sam, any damned way you look at it.'

Sam agreed again. 'Yes sir, for a fact it is.'

'You want to ride with us in the morning?'

Sam Bolt stubbed out his smoke in a cut-off tomato can on the table for that purpose. He gazed thoughtfully across the table. 'You don't owe me anything for one day's work, Mister Beam,' he said, and got slowly to his feet, the ivory handle of his sixgun bumping wood as he arose. 'I got something else to do tomorrow, and I can't hardly ask for the day off when I only been on the ranch one day, so I better quit.'

Jake Beam turned his head, as did the cook, to watch Sam Bolt leave the cookshack, neither of them with a word to say.

Later, when Sam was out behind the barn snaking out his personal horse to be put into a separate corral for easy catching in the morning, Mister Beam went over to the bunkhouse.

Sam had the horse apart and was leaning on the pole gate smoking his final quirley of the day, when Morales, Buford and Carnes came up silently and soberly and also leaned, looking in at the horse. Abel eventually turned a little as he said, 'Sam; what difference does it make whether the law hangs that son of a bitch, or we do it?'

Bolt shrugged. 'None, I guess. He'll go to hell either way, won't he?'

'Yeah, for a fact. Then why'd you quit, and why do you figure to ride into town tomorrow and see Marshal Hedrich?'

Bolt turned slightly, trickling smoke and studying them. They were out here because Mister Beam had told them of the conversation at the cookshack. A fair guess would be that they were not going to allow him to ride away.

'I'm not goin' to see Tom Hedrich. I'm goin' over there to buy a horse ... Maybe I'll see Tom. A lot of things have happened today, Abel. I guess I'm not a fast thinker. For the time being I'm trying to puzzle through. But right now, standin' out here, it's not my idea to see Tom Hedrich.'

The lanky tophand's broad brow furrowed. He was having no better luck at understanding the new hand than his employer had had. Juan Morales said, 'You better stay, Sam.'

The three of them were not as hostile to him as they were determined. Mister Beam had explained to them at the bunkhouse what they would do tomorrow. They were willing because they believed it was the right thing to do, because they had all liked Charley, and because they were loyal to the brand they rode for.

Sam leaned on the gate gazing at them. He could, he was certain, out-gun any single one of them. He also knew no man could out-gun three men at close range. But that was not what kept him slouching there looking at them. None of this was worth killing for.

As for Baker, he had ambiguous feelings. For one thing if Baker was a bushwhacker, Sam Bolt would eat his hat. For another thing, he had thought about the dying woman quite a bit on the ride back today. If Mister Beam hanged her man, he would do it where she would see it being done. Mister Beam might be a fair man, according to range viewpoints, but he was also a callous man; most rangemen of his age and background were.

Finally, then what would happen to her?

Morales was normally a very patient individual, but this kind of affair made his nerves crawl and he wanted to get it over with. 'Go in the barn,' he said, with both hands hanging loosely at his sides, and his black eyes fixed upon Sam's face.

Bolt made no move to obey as he considered the dark man. 'There is no proof, as far as I know. Mister Beam named Baker, but that was all . . . Hell you don't want to ride out tomorrow and hang some poor son of a bitch who didn't kill anyone.'

Morales did not move. 'There is proof. I found where he stood in some trees waitin' for us when we rode down there on his tracks lookin' for him. He stood there waiting for us.

He levered up a fresh load into his carbine, and he spit blood . . . We turned back before we got close because the light was failing. That's proof.'

Sam straightened up a little off the gate looking steadily at Morales. 'Spit blood?'

'Yes. I fetched back some dirt. We put hot water over it. It was blood, Sam.'

Cotton Buford had been silent up until now. 'We figured he was a lunger, Sam.'

For a long time Sam said nothing, just looked at them, then he spoke again to Juan Morales. 'He spit blood—for a fact?'

'Yes. I just told you he did.'

'You found this place and read the sign?'

'Yes.'

'Who was with him?'

'No one. He was alone.'

Sam gazed steadily at Morales. 'You're sure of that? You're good enough at reading sign to swear he was alone?'

Juan Morales's eyes widened. There was a drop in his voice when he answered. 'I'll tell you something, Sam. I been reading sign all my life. I think you are trying to say I was lying about what I saw.'

Abel and Cotton looked from Sam to Morales, and when Sam spoke again they continued to look at the *vaquero*. They knew Juan Morales a lot better than Sam did.

'I'm not trying to say anything of the kind,'

Sam told Morales. 'If you're as good as you say, then there is something wrong.'

'*Que?* What is wrong?'

'Baker isn't a lunger, Morales. He don't spit blood. But . . .'

Morales had the advantage of darkness when he drew. He also had another advantage, Sam did not know the *vaquero*'s temperament. Morales cocked the gun. 'Go into the barn,' he said. 'If you don't move, I am going to kill you . . . You called me a liar. No one calls me a liar.'

Sam moved slowly off the gate, turning in the direction of the barn's rear opening. Abel strolled ahead and lifted away the ivory-handled sixgun. He and Cotton let Morales remain directly behind the unarmed man.

It was dark inside the barn, but they had all been out in the night long enough so that their eyes were more or less accustomed to gloom. Even so, Morales ordered Sam to halt a yard past the doorway while Abel and Cotton went after the pigging-strings off their saddles.

They tied Sam's hands behind his back then pushed him to the ground with his shoulders against a stall door, and bound his ankles.

Finally, Morales eased down the hammer and holstered his Colt. He stood in front, gazing downward without saying a word. Sam's impression was that Morales was not a man it would ever be easy to appease.

Cotton and Abel stood there too, but they

70

spoke. Cotton said, 'I can't figure you out, Sam. You been around long enough to know what happens to bushwhackers. I'd have guessed you'd maybe pulled on a few hang-ropes in your time.'

Sam did not deny it. 'Guilty men, Cotton.'

'Well, what in the hell do you think this son of a bitch is? Juan knows sign, and we know what we saw happen right here in the yard.'

'I tried to tell you out there, Cotton: if there was blood where he was standing in among the trees, it wasn't Baker because he isn't a lunger.'

'How do you know he isn't?'

Juan Morales broke in, speaking in a flat tone of voice. 'I tell you how he knows. How could he know anything about Baker unless he knew the son of a bitch? I tell you what I think—we ought to hang Sam first, before we go find the other one. I tell you how it looks to me; if he is a friend of Baker's, then maybe he knew, maybe he even helped.'

Jake Beam appeared out front carrying a lantern. He peered from the front doorway, then walked down holding his lantern high enough so that he could see the bound man on the stone-like earthen floor of his barn.

Not a word was spoken for a long time, until Mister Beam lowered the lantern a little and jerked his head as he said, 'Is he tied right good?'

Abel answered. 'He ain't going anywhere,

71

Mister Beam.'

'All right; let's get some sleep because we'll be on our way before sunup.'

Morales spoke. 'He knows Baker. He told us Baker isn't a lunger. The only way he'd know that, Mister Beam, was if him and Baker was friends ... I tell you what I think; maybe he helped Baker kill Charley. I think we ought to hang him first.'

Jake Beam had not taken his eyes off Sam Bolt during the *vaquero's* statement. He simply turned to lead the way out of the barn. His men followed in silence, all but Juan Morales relieved that their employer had not agreed with Morales about a hanging.

CHAPTER EIGHT

ONE MAN'S CONVICTION

It got cold in the late night, with darkness like the inside of a cave everywhere except beyond the rear barn opening where Sam Bolt could see stars against the westerly rims. And there was absolute silence, not even the horses out back in the corrals were moving. Sam longed for a smoke, otherwise, excepting for the creeping chill, he did not feel too badly. If a man had to spend a night trussed like a calf, he could be a lot more philosophically resigned on a full gut, and Sam had that.

When the chill turned into downright cold, Sam heard someone shuffling toward him from out front and waited. When the silhouette appeared he knew who the visitor was. The Pine Cone *cocinero*. Harold had some hot coffee and a bowl of sweetened oatmeal. He hunkered down and held up the cup. In a half whisper he said, 'Drink . . . It's cold in here.'

Sam drank, then said, 'Yes, and if you're caught out here they'll kick your butt up between your shoulders.'

Harold ignored that and put aside the empty cup. 'This here is hot oat mush . . . It's been fifty years since I spoon fed anyone. Open your mouth.'

Sam obeyed. He was not especially hungry, but he did not want the oatmeal down his shirtfront either and old paunchy Harold had shaking hands. He was attired in an old threadbare blanketcoat, so the shaking was probably not the result of the pre-dawn cold.

When the bowl was empty Sam said, 'I'm obliged to you, Cookie.'

Harold eased around to get more comfortable; squatting when a man had a big paunch made it hard to breathe. He said, 'You damned fool, if you didn't want to ride with them, why didn't you say you would, then slip out in the night and ride away? Why'd you have to shoot off your mouth?'

'I didn't shoot my mouth off, damn it. I thought we were talkin' sense when the Mexican got all fired up and drew on me.'

'Ain't you ever been around greasers before?' Harold asked in a disgusted tone of voice.

'Sure.'

'Well, you didn't act like it. And now what?'

Sam grinned. 'There's makings in my pocket, Harold. You could roll me a smoke if you wanted to.'

'I don't want to. Someone might smell the smoke. Besides, it's an unhealthy habit, blowing smoke out a man's nose and mouth. Why don't you chew like respectable folks do?'

Sam's grin widened. Harold was so upset over what he was doing that he was cranky. 'It's not what I'm going to do,' he said, 'It's what those damned fools are going to do. They're goin' out of here in the morning to hang an innocent man. You know what's going to happen about that? The law will be out here loaded for bear, arrest them all, and they'll get sentenced to prison for murder. Out and out plain everyday murder, Harold . . . That will be the end of Mister Beam . . . It will be the end of the Pine Cone cattle outfit.'

'How do you know this feller is innocent, Sam?'

'I talked to him. In fact I sat up there in the hills where he'd camped beside a spring, and

74

talked with him most of the afternoon. He's not the man who killed your foreman. I know that for an absolute fact. I'd bet my life on it.'

'Is that what you told Mister Beam?'

'... Harold, when was the last time you know of when anyone told Mister Beam anything?'

'Well; he was in the cookhouse last night gettin' coffee, and he told me...'

'I'm telling you Mister Beam wants revenge for the foreman so bad if someone pointed a finger at his mother, he'd hang her ... It's gospel truth, Harold, they're goin' up there in the morning and either kill that man in a gunfight or hang him—and so help me gawd, he did not bushwhack Whitson.'

Harold shifted position again, looked back up toward the yard, where it was beginning to faintly pale out a little, hugged the old coat a little closer and said nothing for a long while, then, with a groan, untied the pigging string which was knotted around Sam Bolt's wrists. He was breathing irregularly as he gathered up the cup and bowl and heaved up to his feet. 'You can do the rest ... Sam, no matter what ... you don't never tell anyone it was me got you free. All right?'

Bolt was already pulling at the ankle bindings. 'My word on it, Harold.' and a moment later when the cook was scuttling toward the front opening, Sam looked after him and said, 'Harold?'

'What?'

'I don't think I can do this by myself.'

Tatum fidgeted, squinting in the direction of both the bunkhouse and the main-house. 'Just saddle up and get the hell on your way,' he said.

'Harold; after they've been fed and ride out, and it's safe, you high-tail it for town and tell the marshal ... Tell him to ride west through the foothills. He'll find the camp. I'll be up there trying to keep a lynching from happening.'

Harold was moving when he said, 'No! I ain't going to do any such a thing. I already done more'n good sense told me to do.' He hastened back in the direction of the cookshack as Sam shook off the last little rope and arose to go out back for his horse.

If he had been a praying man he would have prayed now, because as the darkness began to coldly pale out, the time for Beam and his riders to roll out was close. He saddled up inside the barn and was leading his horse out back when he smelled smoke from the cookhouse stove, and he was rising up over leather when he heard someone leave the bunkhouse, either to wash and shave at the rack out back, or to head for the corral to fork feed to the using horses.

He rode at a quiet walk hoping with all his might that whoever had emerged from the bunkhouse would not see him, and at the same time fought down an almost overwhelming urge to boost his horse over into a lope—except that then he would make noise.

He got almost a mile northward and was safe when he squeezed the horse. He loped all the while the sun was taking its time reaching the easternmost curve of the earth, and by the time it was up there pouring golden brilliance, with very little warmth yet, down over the entire Portales country, Sam was so far along that when he looked back he could no longer see the Pine Cone rooftops.

And finally, he had his smoke.

He thought of paunchy old scanty-haired Harold Tatum and smiled through tangy smoke. He also thought of how much head start he might have. Then he thought of the Bakers up yonder in their wagon-camp, and sighed when he lowered a gloved hand to his right hip; the damned holster was empty and he did not carry a carbine.

Four wolves, with their winter white greying out now that it was summer again, loped up out of an arroyo about a half-mile ahead and turned in the direction of the foothills in an easy lope. They had not seen the mounted man. If he'd had a carbine he would have killed all four of them. If he'd had his sixgun he would have tried to do the same thing. He watched them with every rangeman's animosity showing in his face, and finally, when he whistled and they turned in astonishment and saw him, the leader sprang a foot into the air and came down six feet ahead, with the guard-hairs on his belly brushing the ground. The others did the same, and in their frantic desperation they tried to find another arroyo to duck down into. They expected a fusillade of gunfire. They had every reason to expect it.

Sam stubbed out his smoke on the saddlehorn and watched the wolves abruptly drop from sight down the near side of an erosion gully. If he had been an Indian this encounter would have been some kind of omen. He was not only not an Indian, but he did not believe in omens.

The sun was climbing the last time he sat sideways looking back. There was no sign of them yet, but all that signified was that he had managed to get a good, strong lead on them. They would be along.

With the foothills close, he reined a little to the left in order to enter them about as near the twin fat hillocks with the camp between them as he could. And finally, he slackened off, because from here on speed was not important.

Three black crows which had been sunning in the top of a white oak were startled by the appearance of a mounted man and flung upwards in a raucous complaint like three dark rags.

He smelled the breakfast smoke about the same time his horse did, and aimed in that direction. When he came around the nearest fat hill, he had the camp in view. It was a picturesque scene, the old wagon, the canvas shelter, the skinny, tall man squatting at a stone ring fussing with his first fire of the day.

Sam rode closer, halloed, and when the tall man spun around coming up to his full height as he recognised the rider, Sam looked in the direction of the shelter, but the beautiful woman was not there.

Baker casually stepped to the wagon, took down a carbine and leaned on it. Sam rode up, sighed and swung to the ground. 'I opened a can of worms last night,' he said, looping reins around a wagon wheel. 'Maybe I should have known better, but I didn't. Old Beam is on his way ... I asked some questions ... to get on with it—they didn't like what I had to say and tied me in the barn. I got loose and here I am.'

Ronald Baker continued to watch Sam Bolt and to lean on the carbine. Eventually, still in silence, he moved clear of the vehicle and looked down-country. There were no horsemen in sight. He looked back. 'How far ahead were you?'

Sam had to guess. 'Half-hour. Maybe an hour, but I sort of doubt it.'

'Well; where are they? Look down there. That's flat country. If they was coming they'd at least be in sight by now, wouldn't they?'

Sam moved away from his horse and the wagon while reaching in a shirt pocket for his

79

tobacco sack. There was nothing moving through the golden, brilliant sunlight. He started to build his smoke. In a dry voice he said, 'Don't get impatient, Mister Baker ... How is your wife this morning?'

Instead of replying the tall man went to an upended little sturdy green box and sank down upon it, gazing at Sam Bolt, who was lighting up. Baker finally said, 'Where is your belt-gun?'

'They took it. You got a spare?'

'Yes ... Mister Bolt, to me and my wife you are a real jinx ... Will that horse of yours pull a wagon?'

He would; as a matter of fact Sam had spent a winter breaking the horse to light harness to break line-shack boredom, but as Sam gazed over at the horse he said, 'That's not going to help, Mister Baker. If he was the fastest harness horse in the world, it would not help.' Sam turned as he dropped the quirley to step on it, and remained that way for several moments, before he quietly said, 'I didn't think I had that big a lead on them.'

Baker arose and gazed bitterly southward. 'Four of them. I expected about twice that many, Mister Bolt.'

Sam did not comment. He watched the riders coming forward, made small by the intervening distance, then he turned his back on that unpleasant sight and assessed the camp and the area around it. There were several excellent

80

places to hide; to at least turn bullets, but in this kind of a situation about the best a man could hope for was that they might not be able to make wolf bait out of him for a couple of hours.

He asked where the woman was, and Baker jerked a thumb. 'In the wagon.'

'Bad night?'

'No, as a matter of fact she had a good night, for a change. But she sleeps a lot and I let her do it.'

'Sure. But you better carry her over into the rocks somewhere ... and fetch me that extra belt-gun you got, if you don't mind.'

Ronald Baker stood gazing at the compact, dark-eyed, unshaven rangeman. 'Mister Bolt, we're downright beholden, but why are you willing to side with us? I stole a horse off you yesterday, and you don't even know us.'

Sam crookedly grinned. 'The horse I'd have got back regardless. As for the rest of it: Mister Beam figures to hang you—unless you make a big fight out of it, then he figures to kill you with bullets. He'll do it, Mister Baker, I don't know how well you know cattlemen like Mister Beam, but I know them, and he'll drop you into an unmarked hole by sundown today, if he possibly can do it.'

'That don't answer my questions, Mister Bolt.'

Sam watched the oncoming riders for a moment, speculating that even after they got

81

closer to the foothills, even after Morales led them up Sam Bolt's trail like a bird-dog to the area of the twin hillocks, he would have time enough for what had to be done.

Then he shifted his attention. 'Because I don't think you bushwhacked anyone, an' if I'm right, I guess a man don't have to know someone real well not to like the idea of some stone-set old implacable cowman killing them just because he wants revenge ... Mister Baker; who was with you in the trees down near Rochester when you stood there waiting for the Pine Cone riding crew, after their rangeboss got killed?'

'Mister Bolt, I was not in any trees down there waiting to shoot some rangemen.'

Sam nodded about that. He eyed the tall man for a while then asked another question. 'You never caught the lung fever from your wife?'

'No. It is contagious, I know that, but I've never caught it. A doctor east of here a long ways told me I likely would never catch it if I haven't after nursing Margerie all these years. He also said he wouldn't want to bet any money on that, though.'

Sam shot another glance down where the horsemen were steadily increasing in size. Then he looked back. 'Who shot Mister Beam's rangeboss?'

Baker also turned to watch the oncoming riders, and he did not answer.

CHAPTER NINE

FACE TO FACE

They had a little time, but not enough for Baker
to feed himself and his wife, so he bundled her
in blankets, carried her to a stony place at the
lower side of the westernmost fat hillock,
returned for one of the large canteens and hot
food, then returned to her protected place and
was still over there with her when Sam looked
for them, did not see either of them, and went to
the wagon and picked up Baker's Winchester,
then rummaged until he found the spare sixgun,
and walked up where that sturdy green box was,
and sat down.

Jake Beam was aiming for the slot between
the low hillocks, with Morales out front
watching tracks. Sam had a clear view of each
one of them. They did not come into
Winchester range though, for another ten or
fifteen minutes.

He wanted a cup of the coffee in the pot on
the rocks beside the breakfast fire, but it was
probably too late to go over and fill a cup. He
rubbed beard bristle along his jaw and watched
Juan Morales, who was some yards in advance
of the others. Morales halted, finally, looking up
the grassy place in the direction of the wagon-

camp. He had a carbine balanced across his lap, like a bronco Indian. In fact in colouring he looked rather like one too.

Mister Beam and the others came up and halted, sitting gravely in the rising warmth and sunshine studying the wagon camp. They conferred, Sam could see them leaning toward one another now and then. They could see him—at least they could see someone—sitting on a box in the shade of the wagon. The discussion terminated when Jake Beam said something curt then lifted his rein-hand and eased his mount ahead at a dead walk.

Sam looked over his shoulder again, and this time he saw Baker coming out of the rocks. Sam went back to the tailgate and gestured for the tall man to go back into the rocks. Baker hesitated. Sam made an annoyed gesture, and Baker turned back.

Sam spat, eyed the fragrantly steaming coffee pot, then tested the borrowed sixgun, found that it did not hang in the leather, and eased back the Winchester slide to be sure the gun was armed, then he walked back around into the shade near the green box, and waited.

He could see Mister Beam's face clearly now, which meant that the cowman could also recognise Sam Bolt. They were well within carbine range of one another, but still beyond accurate handgun range.

Beam had a saddle-boot slung forward under

his right-side saddle fender. Beneath his wrinkled black rider's coat of heavy wool he was also wearing a shell-belt and holstered Colt.

Mister Beam came within fifty or sixty feet of the wagon, halted, looped both reins and began to methodically peel off his riding gloves, all the time with his hatbrim-shaded gunmetal eyes fixed upon Sam Bolt. There was not a single compassionate line in his face.

Sam waited. Whatever was to be said, was up to the older man. But whatever it was, he did not believe it was going to end up in gunfire; not when the old man had left his riders back yonder and had come up ahead by himself. But that certainly did not signify that trouble was not coming. What it probably signified was that Jake Beam wanted to spy out the camp and its vicinity.

After pocketing the gloves Mister Beam said, 'You're right handy, Sam. How'd you untie them knots, with your teeth?'

Sam smiled a little. 'I'm here, Mister Beam. That's what matters.'

'Yeah, so I see. Where is the son of a bitch?'

Sam watched the puckered eyes move to the wagon, to the texas, to the fire and surrounding area, then back, and did not utter a word.

'Sam? We're here for him. We'll get him one way or another. But first off, I got some curiosity that needs settling. Can you prove he's not the man who shot Charley?'

85

'I can prove it to my satisfaction, Mister Beam, but you're likely to be a different story.'

Mister Beam placed both hands atop the saddlehorn. 'Try me.'

'I did. I tried all of you yesterday. I dang near got shot for it, and ended up hog-tied in the barn.'

The older man's utterly still, totally unsympathetic eyes bored into the man on the ground. 'What did he do it for, tell me that.'

Sam wanted to glance back in the direction of the rocks, but did not succumb to the urge. He continued to slouch there facing Mister Beam. Over the cowman's shoulder he could see Morales, Abel and Cotton, still back down near the entrance to the little green space between the fat hillocks. As long as they stayed down there, and as long as he and Jake Beam talked, there was not going to be trouble. As he was pulling down a breath before replying to Jake Beam, he had a moment to think of the *cocinero*. If Harold had ridden for the law over in Rochester, this might still end well. But Harold had flatly refused to make that ride, and right at this moment Sam Bolt had a hunch he would not do it. But still, he did not know Harold well enough to know what he might do. But regardless of help which probably would be unable to arrive in time anyway, Sam was on his own.

He said, 'I don't know why your rangeboss

got ambushed. You could probably make a better guess about that than I could.'

'Where is he, Sam?'

'Mister Beam, I'd like to tell you a story.'

'I don't want no gawddamn story. I want the man who bushwhacked Charley Whitson . . . And I'm going to get him.'

Sam barely nodded. 'All right, I won't tell you the story. But I'll tell you something else. I wintered cattle for three years in the north, living alone in a mountain line cabin.'

'I don't give a damn what . . .'

'You shut your damned mouth until I'm finished, Mister Beam . . . All winter long for three years I had nothing to do but trap a little, and practise with guns. For three years. You can't out-shoot me and neither can those riders of yours down yonder. I doubt if all four of you could do it standin' together, but I don't want to test that notion . . . Mister Beam; this is the last time I'm going to say this: The feller who belongs to that wagon and this camp did not kill your rangeboss.'

'No? Then why is he hiding? Or are you killing time with me while he high-tails it? There is only one horse in sight. It's got your saddle on it.'

'He don't have a horse.'

Jake Beam let go a big breath, gazing at the wagon. He did not speak, he simply wagged his head.

'The horse died, Mister Beam ... I'm gettin' thirsty and this is turning out to be about what I figured it would be—a waste of time ... You want a fight? You'll get one. And by the way, I'm not alone here. In fact, the man who owns this wagon and I are not alone.' Sam made a gesture of dismissal. 'You better go back.'

Jake Beam sat a long time gazing at the compactly muscular man leaning on the wagon, with the black-stocked sixgun in his shiny old holster. Sam Bolt had been a puzzle to him right from the start, and this latest exchange had done nothing to ease that condition. But he had one more thing to say.

'I told you I was going to get him. I've never failed to get one yet. What sense does it make for you to get between him an' me? Protecting a murderer is the same as abetting one.'

Sam raised a cuff to wipe sweat off his face. 'I'll tell you the same thing I told someone else. If you kill Baker, you'll sure as hell go to prison for it.'

'Will I? Who is going to ever say what happened to him? You? I don't think so. If you throw in with him, Bolt, you'll go into the same hole in the ground.'

'An' you can justify that?'

'You bet your damned boots I can. Helping a murderer...'

Sam shrugged thick shoulders. 'Go on back, Mister Beam.'

The cowman raised his left hand with the reins in it, at the same time he glanced up the grassy glade, then over to the pair of opposing fat low little hillocks. Finally he began to turn the horse. And he said, 'If you'd tried to find the worst damned place in the world to fort up and make a fight, you couldn't have done any better than right here—down in a damned gully between two hills, with us having a clear field up through this arroyo.'

He rode slowly back down where his riders were sitting in horse-shade waiting. Sam watched him for a while, then also turned to study the terrain. He had never been a soldier, and perhaps Mister Beam had been, otherwise how could he have made such an excellent judgment of the place where the camp was.

Sam waited until Mister Beam and his riders were squatting in a war council, then he strolled over to the rocks where Ronald Baker had rigged a blanket-shelter to keep direct sunlight off his wife. They said nothing as he came into the boulders and selected one to sit on, then smiled at them. The beautiful woman's feverish colour made the very dark, violet shade of her eyes look even darker. She said, 'Is he going to attack us, Mister Bolt?'

'He's going to do something, for a fact, ma'm, because he's got to.' He added nothing to that statement until he could take her husband off a short distance and tell him without her being

89

able to hear them what Mister Beam had said about the place they were in, and Baker listened wearing a slight frown, then turned and cast a narrowed gaze into the near distance where the Pine Cone men were palavering. 'A few sticks of dynamite would change their minds about this being a bad place to defend, wouldn't it?'

Sam said, 'You got some?'

'Six sticks ... Mister Bolt, did you ever see dynamite used with a three-inch cordite fuse?'

Sam never had. In fact all he knew about blasting powder was that it would shatter rock obstructions and lift tree stumps out of the ground. 'Did you ever use the stuff, Mister Baker?'

'Yes. My wife's brother and I filed on a silver mine once. He knew more about blasting than I did, and I've done my share.' The troubled gaze swung back.

Sam thought a while. It seemed to him that in order to use dynamite, they would have to get close, and that meant being shot at. The idea was not only foreign to him, but it also made him feel anxious.

Baker waved an arm in the direction of the easternmost hillock. 'One of us over there with three sticks and crimped fuses, and one of us around behind this here hill, and when they skulk up, light the fuses and pitch the sticks into them.'

Sam sat down upon a slab of grey granite. He

twisted until he could see the Pine Cone men. They had ended their palaver and were preparing to mount up. While he watched two of them rode at a walk toward the east, and the other two rode westerly. Baker, who had also been watching, now said, 'That's their strategy, Mister Bolt. Two to attack from around one little hill, and while we're occupied with that, the other two will slip around from behind the westerly hill. That's called enfilading.'

Sam arose. 'We better rig up those dynamite sticks while they can't see us.' He led the way down to the wagon. When they arrived there Baker climbed up, rummaged in a large wooden chest, climbed back down with a greasy-looking black coil and six sticks of blasting powder encased in red, oiled paper.

Sam sweated, drank from a canteen, and alternately watched the two little hills, and the man calmly working on the tailgate. When Baker handed him three of the sticks and explained how they were to be lighted and hurled, Sam got the impression that Ronald Baker, who was supposed to have been a freighter, had been a number of other things as well. Baker smiled through the sheen of shiny sweat on his face. 'I'd like to be on the west side, Mister Bolt.'

Sam nodded. His wife was in the rocks over there. That was where he belonged in any case. He shoved the sticks inside his shirt and said,

'What will all this do to your wife?'

Baker's gaze instinctively turned in the direction of the sheltered, shaded place, when he replied. 'Nothing. She has been with me when I've used powder before ... Be careful, Mister Bolt.'

Sam did not bother offering reassurances on that score. He had decided to be extremely careful even before he had accepted the sticks. He eyed the tall, thin man. He wanted to say something encouraging, maybe mention that it was not impossible that the Pine Cone cook had ridden to Rochester for aid, but he said nothing. He saw in the tall man's gaze that he had encountered false hope before.

Sam crossed to the underbrush on the lower slope of the eastward hill. He knew his way over there, having come through that same thorny growth the day before when he had tracked down the man who had taken his horse.

It was hotter today though, even though it was not as late in the day. But at least he had tanked up from the canteen, so the same nagging discomfort which had bothered him yesterday did not bother him now.

Other things did, though, as he twisted and turned, working his way through the underbrush. If he had been constituted differently, he would have been full of rage and resentment over Mister Beam's refusal to listen. But that was not his temperament.

As he got down on all fours to squirm through ground-level openings beneath the wide-flaring upper limbs of thorny brush, he worried about whichever two Pine Cone riders were sneaking around his easterly hill, not being close to each other. And he worried about the dynamite sticks, which he had never handled before.

CHAPTER TEN

TWO SURPRISES

The sun was steadily climbing, the sky was pale blue and flawless. If a man could simply sit gazing upwards he would become imbued with a serenity of spirit and soul which went with infinity. It was a pleasant thought. Sam paused in manzanita shade to wipe off sweat and consider the vast vault of heaven. Then he resumed crawling.

When he knew he was not far from the area where the brush thinned out, and eventually terminated altogether, he paused again, this time to check his dynamite sticks. That waxed paper they were encased in was as impervious to sweat as it evidently also was to other varieties of wetness, and Baker had crimped the short length of fuse expertly, none of the fuses had come loose during his progress to the rounded haunch of the easterly hill.

When he was able to finally see ahead and around to his right, the land was empty in eye-hurting sun-brilliance. Sam worried. By his estimate those two Pine Cone Riders should have gotten this far around the back of the hill by now.

He squirmed to the final fringe of underbrush and lay flat, like a lizard, watching and waiting. No riders arrived. He did not see any movement at all, human or animal, until he had been lying there about five minutes. Then a great, fat sidewinder came along. It was as thick as a man's wrist but not very long, and its peculiar sideways motion which projected the scaly body forward was rhythmic. An excited sidewinder moved very fast. This snake was moving steadily toward the shade where Sam was lying, but without speed. It anticipated no trouble.

Sam closed one hand and gouged sand, earth and gravel until he had a fistful, then he waited. The snake's broad, rattler head with the pointed snout remained inches off the ground as the body slithered forward. Sam did not move. When the sidewinder was about six feet distant, Sam abruptly flung the grit, and the surprised snake hesitated for two seconds, which was all that was required for the grit to hit him in his lidless eyes.

He writhed and furiously changed course, the sideways motion carrying him off into the underbrush on Sam's right. Sam shook sweat off his chin and looked to see where the rattler had gone before resuming his other vigil.

They were sitting their horses to his right in the middle distance. They had ridden into sight while Sam had been busy with the snake.

He knew them both: Morales and Abel Carnes. That meant Baker had the old man and Cotton Buford to content with. Sam might have worried about that if he'd had time to worry, because he knew Jake Beam would be experienced at this sort of thing, and from what he knew of Ronald Baker, he could not even successfully steal a horse.

For several moments the Pine Cone riders sat their horses, conversing, then lanky Abel swung to the ground hauling out his carbine. Juan Morales came down more slowly, leaving Sam with the impression that whatever the tophand had decided to do was not something Morales was pleased with, and moments later Sam understood why. They tethered the horses in underbrush and started climbing the hill. Abel was lean and leggy, he was built for this sort of thing, but Morales had shorter legs, his body was thicker, and he climbed awkwardly, using his carbine as a staff.

Sam grunted. The damned fools were going to climb to the top of the low hill where they would command a perfect view of the grassy vale between the two hills where the wagon camp was. They could have accomplished the same thing with much less sweat simply by riding around to the low slope where Sam was lying.

He swore under his breath and back-crawled until he was in thick underbrush again, then he turned, stood upright and also began climbing toward the crest. He made better time because he knew he had to. Abel and Morales paused often to suck air. They had no reason to believe there was a need to get up there first.

Sam's heart was working hard. He climbed with his mouth open and with sweat running in rivulets beneath his clothing. It had been Sam Bolt's feeling for years that the reason the Good Lord gave a man two legs and a fair-sized brain, and a horse four legs and a little tiny brain, was so that the man could sit on the horse and make him do things like climb hills on hot days.

He finally halted where two scrub pine trees grew. There was no more than perhaps another three hundred feet to go. There were several more of those scrub pines growing upon the partially flat topout of the hill, and there was almost no underbrush up there.

Thirst became a problem as the sun continued serenely upon its overhead arc. Sam looked down into the vale. There was no movement down there. He could see over into the rocks where Baker had put his wife, and see the blanket-shelter he had made for her.

When he started upwards again he heard rattling small stones on his left and perhaps down the far hillside a hundred yards, which was reassuring because he interpreted it to mean that the Pine Cone men would not reach the topout before he did. It was a reasonable surmise, but it happened also to be wrong.

Finally, the last time Sam stopped, he could see along the top of the hill over as far as the scrub pine trees. There was a huge bird's nest in the very top of one of the trees. It was made of large twigs, was untidy and not very old. He had seen eagle's nests before, and if he had been an Indian this particular nest would have kept him rooted in place, because, although it was obviously this season's nest, most likely with either eggs or chicks in it, there were no parent eagles up there, or anywhere else in view.

He was not an Indian. He began working his way ahead once more, utilising the flourishing stands of tall, thick underbrush as protection, and except for that he probably would have walked right down Abel Carnes's gunbarrel, because the tall man was standing in tree-shade, motionless and therefore not noticeable, positioned so that he could look down into the vale, profiled to Sam Bolt.

Abel had his saddlegun hooked carelessly in the crook of a bent arm. Behind him, down the far side of the hill, more gravel rattled as Morales toiled upwards, a good hundred yards in the wake of Abel Carnes. It had been Morales's noise Sam had heard, and misread.

Sam let his breath out slowly, and even more slowly sank to his haunches amid the underbrush where shade created a pattern of speckled camouflage which further concealed him.

Abel finally left off studying the vale and turned back to watch for Juan Morales. Sam lifted out his handgun. The range was a little long, but he could have shot Carnes. Morales finally emerged over the rounded lip of the topout, sweat-drenched and breathless. He leaned on his carbine, shook off water, and pulled in large sweeps of air while gazing at the tophand. When he was able to speak, he said, 'I don't do this again,' and Abel shrugged, turned and started back across the topout to the place where he had been looking down at the wagon camp. Morales followed, then sank to one knee leaning on his saddlegun to also look down there.

Sam fished one of the waterproof sticks from inside his shirt, placed it on the ground, and was raising his cocked Colt to challenge the Pine Cone men, when Abel suddenly turned back toward tree-shade with Morales following. They had protection now. Sam cursed. He should have been faster. They had been completely exposed over on the western lip of the topout. He waited until he could see them fairly well, then sang out.

'Abel! Morales!'

In a second they were invisible, flat out over there among the trees.

'This is Sam Bolt! Walk out of the trees and leave your guns behind!'

There was not a sound. Neither was there movement, which Sam had not expected.

'Abel—listen to me—I'm goin' to blow you to Kingdom Come if you don't come out!'

They had been trying to place his position by the sound of his voice, and Morales thought he had the range. He fired his saddlegun. Sam heard the bullet slash through underbrush a yard to his left. He saw the rank gunsmoke motionless in the still, heavy air.

He lit the end of the fuse, waited until it was furiously sputtering, then heaved it—not into the trees, but down the west side of the topout, where the Pine Cone men had been toiling upwards minutes earlier.

The explosion even stunned Sam. Rocks, earth, scraps of underbrush, flew in all directions, the cloud of dust was much larger than Sam had thought it would be, and the noise was deafening. Even the echoes, one upon the other, were unnerving. To the men among the scrub pines, who were closer to the point of detonation, it must have been a terrifying experience.

While there were still diminishing echoes Sam

called again. 'Next one is right down your damned throats ... Come out and leave the guns behind!'

They obeyed. This time Morales was out ahead with both arms stretched above his head. Abel's arms were also raised, but not as stiffly.

Sam let them stand out in the sun for a while before ordering them to shed their boots and turn their pockets inside out. Morales had a boot-knife but Abel had no concealed weapons, and when the burnt-powder-scented silence finally returned, he calmly said, 'Bolt—what the hell was that?'

'A stick of dynamite. I didn't want to blow you up, Abel, just shake you up.'

Sam arose and walked out where they could see him. He was holding the cocked sixgun. 'Where is Mister Beam?' he asked, and when they stood looking at him mutely, he leathered his sixgun, rolled and lit a smoke, then smiled at them. He brought out another stick of dynamite and said, 'The last time: Where is old Beam and Cotton?'

He held the lighted end of his cigarette two inches from the fuse and Morales caved in. 'Over behind the other hill ... You know much about dynamite? Move that smoke farther away; it don't have to be fire, just enough heat can ignite that fuse.'

Sam moved the cigarette away. He said, 'Let's get your boots and walk down to the

100

wagon ... Either one of you try and pick up a gun, I'll break your legs. Let's go.'

The guns were lying in shade, and as Sam's prisoners leaned on trees to tug on their boots, Abel said, 'He won't get away.'

Sam watched Morales more closely than he watched the tophand, but Morales had not recovered from being stunned by the explosion. He pulled on his boots and arose, waiting for whatever came next. He was different from what he had been; more wary now.

Abel sighed and re-set his hat. 'I told Mister Beam you'd think of something.' Abel, was broodingly gazing down the brushy sidehill as he spoke. 'Sam, you're a damned fool. Mister Beam will get him, take my word for it ... I don't give a damn what you do. I've worked for him long enough to know—he don't never give up on something like this.' Abel turned a dispassionate look toward Sam Bolt. 'Maybe the dynamite will slow him a little—but you've lost anyway.'

Sam considered them, and growled for Morales to get over beside the tophand before he said, 'Why have I lost, Abel?'

'Because before we left the yard Mister Beam sent Harold down to Rochester to get Marshal Hedrich and a posse. By now they'll be heading this way.'

Sam gazed a long time at the tophand, then gestured with the sixgun. 'Start down the hill,

101

and keep out of the brush. Stay together ...
Morales, don't do anything foolish. You
understand?'

The *vaquero* bobbed his head, then turned to
stay close as the tophand began the descent,
picking his footing carefully, and obeying Sam
Bolt's order to avoid the thickets as much as he
could.

Abel's attitude was detached. He moved
slowly and deliberately, the way a man would
who had been beaten and who accepted that
condition because he had not initially had much
zeal about what he had been ordered to do.

Juan Morales looked back a few times. Sam
was holding the cocked sixgun again. He was
too close for Morales to try and dive into the
thick brush. But the *vaquero's* attitude was not
as indifferent as was the attitude of the tophand.
Morales expected to be paid back for his action
against Sam Bolt back in the ranch yard. That
was how he thought. But the farther down the
sidehill they got, the less opportunity there was
for him to escape, and he feared his captor's
sixgun much less than he feared having another
of those dynamite sticks thrown in his direction.

They reached the final fringe of brush and
ploughed through into the grassy vale, less than
a hundred yards from the wagon, when a
reverberating explosion made dust fall from
shaken leaves in the underbrush behind them.
They stopped and Morales's eyes rolled.

The explosion had come from around behind the far hilloock, lower, close to ground-level back there, which made Sam think that Mister Beam and Cotton Buford had been stalking the camp from the lower north side of the hill. He spat, gestured, and when his prisoners started toward the wagon, there was a noticeably acrid scent to the air around them.

At the wagon, Sam reached for the hanging canteen, drank deeply, then tossed the canteen to Abel Carnes, who also drank. Morales, the last of them to drink, replaced the canteen on its wagon-side hook, then lifted his hat and waited for roiled air to cool his head.

CHAPTER ELEVEN

SAVAGE MEN

After that distant explosion there was neither sound nor movement and that worried Sam. He made his prisoners lie belly-down, found rope to tie them with, then rolled them like logs beneath the wagon where they would be out of the sun's direct heat.

Abel Carnes looked up and said, 'If he killed them the law'll hang him so high birds won't even be able to make nests in his hair.'

Sam's retort was curt. 'Not for self-defence.'

'You'll see. Hedrich sure as hell was close enough to hear that.'

Sam eyed them in silence for a moment, then started in the direction of the rocks where Baker's wife was lying in hot shade. When he got over there she was patting her face with a wet handkerchief and looked out at him, her gaze surprisingly serene for a woman whose husband might be dead, but maybe that kind of detachment was part of the dying process. He smiled, said nothing, and walked around through the rocks, found her husband's boot-tracks in the shale and dust, and slackened pace only when he was beginning to follow out the curve of the hill about a hundred feet above the flatter ground.

The smell of ancient dust and burned powder was strong. Sam had a sudden unpleasant thought: What would happen if the two sticks inside his shirt were suddenly detonated. What little he knew about dynamite about half convinced him this could not happen, unless there was fire to light the fuses. Then he abandoned those thoughts because if he were wrong, and the sticks could be detonated some way, he would not even know it.

He dropped flat at the scrape of leather over rock somewhere to his left. The sixgun came out and up, but he did not cock it. That sound too, would carry.

There was not as much brush on this lower

slope as there had been upon the other hill, and there was a deep erosion gully bisecting the gritty slope. The brush would not conceal him but the arroyo would. He started to crawl. He only had a general idea where the other man was. He also doubted that he would be able to roll down into the gully before the other man saw him. But anything was better than just lying there with a very poor screen of brush between him and whoever that was sneaking down in his direction.

When the next sound of someone coming arrived, Sam halted dead-still. The other man had evidently not been coming down where Sam had been lying, he had instead been crossing through the brush on an angle which would place him between Sam and the arroyo.

Sam was unmindful of dripping sweat now. He looked desperately for concealment. There was none. Two spindly chaparral bushes grew near the lip of the arroyo, and that was all. He eased up onto one knee looking intently for the other man. If it turned out to be Baker, fine, but the odds were two to one against that possibility. He saw nothing and the silence was deeper than ever. There was a haziness to the air which probably was the result of that dynamite blast.

Sam stood up in a low crouch and started for the arroyo. He moved slightly uphill to avoid the chaparral, and having reached the crumbly edge, holstered his weapon and dropped forward ready to roll downward. At that exact moment a man's hat, then his two hands and his head, appeared over the lip of crumbly earth. Sam saw the sixgun in one of the hands as the man strained to pull himself upwards. Their eyes met in mutual astonishment. Sam snarled and dropped forward. Cotton Buford also reacted instantly. He let go with both hands to fall backwards. He should have tried to drop sidewards. Sam landed atop him and they rolled to the bottom of the gully.

Cotton arched with all his strength to pitch Sam off, and partially succeeded because Sam was leaning sideways reaching for Buford's gun-wrist. He caught it in his left hand, then they rolled and Cotton struck out, grunting with the effort. The blow was low, and although it landed squarely, there was no real power behind it. Sam leaned, got both hands around Buford's gun-wrist, hauled the arm upwards then slammed it violently downward. He did that three times, raising it higher each time, and piling more body-weight behind it each time he brought it down. Cotton's fingers flexed, the gun fell away, and as Sam rocked back to regain balance Cotton hit him under the right ear, and this time there was power in the strike.

Sam was temporarily stunned. He dropped forward in an instinctive move to smother the man beneath him, but Buford rolled desperately. Sam fell off, Buford jumped up and turned looking for his gun. Sam turned completely over and came up to one knee, his mind and vision clearing. He saw Cotton lunge for the gun and reached downwards. His holster was empty.

Without consciously thinking, Sam sprang up and catapulted forward, striking Cotton as Buford was closing his hand around his sixgun. They went down, dust flew, and Sam groped frantically for the gun-wrist again. This time, Buford anticipated him, swung his right arm above his head, and struck downward with it. The pain of a steel barrel across his left shoulder, smashing flesh and grinding over bone, was excruciating. Sam's mind was totally cleared by the pain. He pushed upwards to prevent the second blow from landing as hard, then he hurled all his weight forward and caught the gun-arm. Cotton was fast and frantic, but he was on his back struggling against heavier weight, and no longer had leverage to strike downward with the gun.

Sam forced the arm backwards and sideways until Cotton choked with pain, then Sam prised the gun loose and rocked back, he cocked the weapon and put the barrel beneath Cotton Buford's chin, and watched the younger man's pale eyes widen in expectation. Cotton stopped struggling. Sam gulped air and did not move for a long time. His shoulder hurt and his lungs were afire. He watched terror congeal on the cowboy's face, and said, 'I ought to blow your damned head off.'

Cotton ran his words together in a wheezing plea. 'Don't! I give. I wasn't goin' to shoot no one. I was tryin' to get back to the horses. Jesus...!'

Sam eased away, got to his feet still pointing the cocked Colt at the straw-haired cowboy. The pain was worse now. He did not believe his collarbone was broken, but it would not have hurt any worse if it had been. His shirt was torn, his hat was gone, and there was a thin flung-back streamer of blood at the corner of his mouth. Afterwards, he was never clear about how he had got that injury, but right at this moment he was not aware he had it.

'Get up,' he told Buford, and as the battered younger man rolled up to his feet, he flinched from a pain in his right side, arm and shoulder. He looked even worse. In an unsteady voice he said, 'I was tryin' to get away. That's the truth. That explosion rolled me down the hill. I tried to hide in the arroyo.'

'Where is Jake Beam?'

Cotton did not know. 'He was south of me, followin' me around the slope, when that explosion went off ... Likely he got blowed to hell. Did you do that—what was it, dynamite?'

Sam found his sixgun in the dirt where they had tumbled together, holstered it, picked up his hat and gestured with the gun. 'Climb out of here.'

Cotton turned to obey. He was unable to do it, so Sam got below and boosted, hard, then as Cotton reached the upper area, Sam aimed the gun at him and said, 'Give me your hand.' He kept the gun aimed during the time when Cotton strained hard to pull Sam upwards.

But there was no fight left in the younger man. He was not only injured, he was confused and weak. He sank to the ground while Sam stood looking around. Jake Beam was around there somewhere, maybe hurt, and so was Ronald Baker. If he went searching for them he would have to take Cotton with him, and while he did not fear an attack from the badly beaten cowboy, in his present shape Buford would stumble around making noise. Sam sighed, shoved Cotton's gun into his waistband and growled, 'Get up and start walking.'

They went back the way Sam had come, Buford's shirt-tail hanging, his hair awry, his face bruised, his back, finally, making walking painful for him, his pale eyes aimlessly moving.

Sam growled at his prisoner so that when they came around toward the vale, they were a couple of hundred yards south of the rocks where Baker's wife was lying. They were in fact almost exactly opposite the wagon when they left the sidehill and walked out into the grass.

The silence was deep, the atmosphere still had dust and that rank scent to it. The sun was changing colour, shading toward a deeper hue as the afternoon advanced, but the heat was still there as Sam Bolt herded his prisoner up to the wagon, and with the two bound men beneath staring, he shoved Buford to the ground and went after rope to tie him with.

He worked in disgruntled silence and when he was finished he looked squarely at the light-haired rangerider. 'Those two fellers who quit: if you and Morales had a lick of sense you would have quit too.'

Cotton was in pain. It showed in his face. But his mind was clear. 'Just find my horse,' he told Sam Bolt. 'Mister Beam don't even have to pay me . . . I don't never want to even ride through this damned country again.'

Sam rolled him under the wagon beside the other two, and went after the canteen. The water was almost hot, but it was wet, which was all that really mattered. Then he pulled off his old hat, beat dust out of it, punched it into some semblance of its original shape and pulled it forward to shield his eyes.

He looked toward the westerly hill, saw nothing, heard nothing, and sat down on the little green box to roll and light a cigarette. His shoulder shot pain all the way through him each time he moved that arm. His mouth was swelling slightly on one side, and his ribs hurt. He shoved his left hand inside his shirt to relieve the shoulder of at least that much weight, and

110

smoked. If he knew where Baker cached his whiskey he probably would have searched for it.

From the coolness beneath the wagon Abel Carnes said, 'Sam ... Mister Beam met his match.'

Bolt inhaled, exhaled, and replied without looking around. 'Shut up. You sons of bitches ... When I'm up to it, I'm goin' to stand each one of you up, count three, then beat you to the draw.'

Abel was not cowed. 'Where is Mister Beam?'

'I hope the old bastard is shovelling coal. If he isn't, I'm goin' to stand him up too.' Sam dropped the smoke and smashed it underfoot.

'Sam ...'

'Abel, I told you to shut up.'

'All right.'

'What were you going to say?'

'It's kind of dry, lyin' under here.'

'You want some water?'

'Yeah.'

'Shut up and go to hell.'

Abel did not speak again. Neither did the other two. Sam ached in places he had never ached before, but sitting in the shade, with water to drink, and with the heat finally beginning to diminish, his body began to recover. It would still be a long while before he danced a fandango and he knew it, but just sitting there quietly, in the silence, allowing his battered carcass to achieve some measure of recovery, was pleasant, and as long as he did not move, his shoulder did not hurt the way it had earlier.

He thought about Ronald Baker. Unless something had gone wrong around the hillside, he probably should have come back by now.

He also thought of Jake Beam, and in this case, he hoped something had gone wrong. Finally, he thought of the dying woman, and that made him stir a little. She might be out of water, and for a fact she'd had nothing to eat in a long time.

He arose, the aching started again, he looked in the direction of the rocks, which were in shade now, and saw movement where someone was making waves in the shadows. It was not the violet-eyed woman. The silhouette was too thick and tall.

He went around to the tailgate and leaned there, watching. It was not Mister Beam either. Beam was not as tall. Sam glanced in the wagon, saw the burlap-wrapped jug beneath a set of harness, studied it for a moment, figured out a way to reach it with one hand without having to climb over the tailgate, and moved to the wagon's far side.

It was rye whiskey. He winced as he lifted the jug, swallowed three times, placed the jug back among the leather straps, and leaned a while, until the pleasant sensation ran out to all his fingers and toes, then he turned in the direction of the rocks, shoving his left hand into his shirt again as he progressed. The shoulder hardly hurt at all as long as the weight of the arm did not pull at it.

Some veil-like streamer clouds were edging on a diagonal course across the pale sky, and the sun, which was no more than a third of the way downward toward some very distant uneven barren peaks, was like dull copper; reddish and tarnished brown.

A little vagrant breeze came down through the vale from the north, the first cooling freshet to reach this place since Sam Bolt had arrived up here, and two bald eagles soared in from the east on motionless wings to circle, and continue to circle that scrub pine atop the eastern hillock where that haphazard, untidy large nest was.

CHAPTER TWELVE

IN THE WAGON

Baker was feeding his wife from a tin plate of food left over from breakfast, and as Sam sat down Baker looked at him. Sam said, 'I got three tied under the wagon. Where is Beam?'

Baker went on feeding the woman as he replied, 'I don't know, but wherever he is, he's on foot. That blast made their horses break

113

away. The last I saw, they were running southward scairt half out of their wits. I didn't know they were in the brush nearby when I saw two men and tossed the powder.'

Sam nodded. 'You did more than scare the horses. One of them, they call him Cotton, got rolled down the hill.'

For a moment there was silence while Sam watched the tall man gently feed his wife. The next words came from the woman, when she put her bright gaze upon Sam Bolt.

'You've been injured. Ron has a medicine box at the wagon.'

He smiled at her. 'I found it, ma'm. It was in a jug wrapped with burlap. How do you feel?'

'Fine,' she replied. 'Now that both of you are here.'

Sam eyed the cold food. 'You need decent grub and a decent bed ... My horse will work between shafts ... Abel, Beam's tophand, told me Marshal Hedrich is coming up here. I guess we might as well get the horse hitched and start for town, whether he finds us or not ... But he will; those dynamite blasts made enough racket to raise the dead.'

The woman lay back with closed eyes and Sam jerked his head for her husband to follow him. They walked out a ways then Sam said, 'If Jake Beam got blown up, it was self-defence. But in this country that might not mean a lot, you bein' a stranger under suspicion and all. But

114

what matters right now is that we get her down where the doctor can look after her. All right?'

Baker agreed. 'All right. But the doctors have all said . . .'

'Never mind that, Mister Baker. I've met my share of them, an' maybe one out of ten is right.'

They went down to the wagon, pitched Sam's riding outfit into the wagon, led his horse around front and Baker held up the shafts as Sam backed the horse between them. From beneath the wagon someone said, 'Get us out from under here.' Sam ignored that plea, buckled the harness into place, ran both shafts through the leather loops, then patted his horse, which had accepted this altered situation with philosophical indifference. Like many horses with a nickel's worth of age on them, if something did not hurt them, they would obey the requirements of the two-legged creatures Mother Nature, or Fate, or someone anyway, had made them subservient to.

Ronald Baker looked toward the shaded rocks, but Sam interrupted his thoughts. 'We'll drive over and lift her in. Carryin' her this far can't be good for her . . . Tell me something, Mister Baker; how long has she had the lung fever?'

'Six years . . . She won't make the seventh year, Mister Bolt.'

Sam said, 'You make me uncomfortable. Quit tryin' to bury her . . . Lend me a hand with these sons of bitches.'

Baker had to do most of the tugging and lifting. Sam's left shoulder gave out when he bent to help lift Carnes. Baker was a strong man, for all his thinness, or maybe he was simply motivated to get away from this place. None of the captives spoke as they were lugged around and pitched over the tailgate, but Juan Morales kept watching Sam, and when Bolt saw this, he turned on the Mexican. 'If you had a brain, you'd take it out and play with it. Back at the yard, in the barn, if these other two idiots hadn't listened to you, none of this would have happened.'

Morales was expressionless. He said, 'You're right. The three of us wouldn't be tied right now ... But Charley Whitson was a good man, a friend.'

Sam went around and with his right arm extended, retrieved the burlap-covered jug again, and hoisted it. As he was replacing it and saw Morales watching, he said, 'My pappy told me when I was a kid that a good way to figure out if someone has a brain is to listen to their judgments. If they pass a judgment after hearing just one side of something, they don't have. You don't have.' He wiped water from his eyes before saying, 'Mister Baker; spit.'

The tall man blinked.

'Spit, damn it. Cough and spit.'

Baker coughed and expectorated. Sam went

116

around to the tailgate, grabbed the bound *vaquero* with his right hand and wrenched him around. 'Look,' he commanded. 'Look down there. You see blood where he spit?'

Morales was on his belly with his head over the tailgate. He looked down because he had to. Sam told Baker to expectorate again, and this time the skinny man obeyed without delay. Sam grabbed Morales by the scruff of the neck and pushed his head lower. 'See any blood?'

Morales said, 'No.'

Sam rolled him back into the wagon. 'You know what I'm talking about?'

'No.'

'You found blood where that bushwhacker waited in the trees down near Rochester ... Mister Beam took that up, and came up here to kill this skinny feller. Morales, you brainless bastard, this is what I tried to tell you fellers last night. Beam was going after the wrong man. This feller isn't a lunger ... His wife over yonder in the rocks—she is a lunger and spits blood. But she's as weak as a kitten. She didn't kill your friend. She could not even have sat a horse that long, to ride over to the yard, shoot someone, then ride back as far as Rochester. Now do you know what I was trying to tell you?'

Juan Morales looked a long time at Sam, then turned his eyes upon the tall, thin man. He may have wanted to speak, but Abel spoke first. He and Cotton had taken all this in. Abel said,

'Who, then?'

Sam turned toward the front of the wagon where his horse was patiently standing. 'You boys still don't understand,' he said, climbing to the spring-seat and reaching for the lines. 'Right here and now, who killed your foreman isn't the issue; you wanted to kill Baker. You'd have done it too, if you could have.' He talked to his horse and the wagon began to move, to turn up across the grassy place in the direction of the rocks. 'You half-wit sons of bitches didn't even try to find out if there was more to it than old Beam's wrong judgment. You just wanted to kill someone you never saw before.'

Abel started to say something. Sam was driving toward the rocks and snarled at the tophand. 'Shut up. You turn my stomach. The lot of you. Just shut up and keep shut up.'

They had to push the captives aside to lift Baker's wife up behind the spring-seat, where it was supposed to be less rough and bumpy. Baker arranged her pallet and knelt holding her hand with four sets of eyes fixed upon them both. Abel finally raised his head a little as though to speak, and Sam pointed a rigid finger at him. He did not speak. He did not have to, Abel understood and lowered his head.

Sam drove down the vale steering closer to the eastern hillock because the sub-irrigated ground in the middle of the swale was soft. His horse was pulling a fair load; Sam wanted to favour

118

him every way he could. The horse only weighed a little over nine hundred pounds. What he was willingly doing now by all rights should have been done by a horse which weighed at least twelve hundred pounds.

Baker watered each of the prisoners from one of the canteens and when they came upon an unexpected seepage spring on the east side of the vale shortly before they got away from the twin hillocks. Sam set the binders, climbed down and watered his horse.

The heat was leaving, visibility was diminishing, and as Sam leaned across his horse looking back, he thought there was movement to the west, around where the fat, low hill had grass instead of chaparral. He rolled a smoke, listened to his horse tanking up, lit the quirley and continued to watch. By the time the horse was finished Sam was sure he had seen movement. He also had a notion what might be making it. A solitary man on foot.

He said, 'Mister Baker, keep an eye on things,' and started walking. The woman and tied prisoners could not see over the wagon side, but Baker could, and eventually, as he watched Sam Bolt, he saw the thing which had attracted Sam's attention. He watched it for a moment, then groped for his carbine and dropped down over the tailgate. He hesitated. Three sets of eyes were fixed on him. He turned, saw the looks, and swore under his breath. He would remain with the wagon, but he remained out there beyond the tailgate with the carbine, watching as Sam began to blend with the oncoming dusk.

Sam crossed about seventy yards of spongy ground then halted, lifted out his sixgun and aimed it directly at the man another half dozen or so yards in front of him. The man was leaning on a crooked stick. He was hatless, and even in that poor light it was apparent that he could not walk very well.

Sam said, 'Drop your gun.'

The man clutching his stick with both hands answered thickly. 'I don't have a gun ... Mister Bolt, I got a busted leg.'

Sam did not lower the Colt. 'You old son of a bitch, if you didn't already have one, I'd give you one. Take off your coat and drop it.'

Jake Beam obeyed awkwardly. He was wearing a shell-belt but his holster was indeed empty. He was also hatless and there was blood on one side of his face where the dynamite blast had hurled him headlong into sharp rock. He looked more dead than alive as he clutched his staff and waited.

Sam leathered his weapon and walked on up. Jake Beam's eyes were sunken, their expression was cloudy as though they did not focus very well. He said, 'I think one of my riders is dead, back yonder. I saw him go up into the air and fall.'

120

Sam sighed. His shoulder was hurting again so he shoved the arm inside his shirt. 'He isn't dead. Neither are Morales or Carnes. They're tied up and lying in that wagon ... Throw down that stick and lean on me.'

'I can't. My leg is busted.'

Sam got his good right arm around the older man's waist and tightened his hold. 'Now drop the stick.' Mister Beam obeyed. They started back very slowly. Jake Beam raised one thick arm to Sam's shoulder and hopped. He did not make a sound although he had to be in great pain.

Baker came out to assist, and when they got Mister Beam up to the tailgate Sam eased off and growled, 'My horse isn't going to haul all this damned dead weight.' He turned on Abel and Morales. 'You two will walk.' He climbed up, untied their ankles and roughly shoved them over the tailgate to the ground. Then he helped Baker boost Mister Beam up and while Baker was making the old cowman comfortable, Sam put slipknotted ropes around the necks of the tophand and the *vaquero*, made the ends fast to the tailgate chains, and gazed at the silent men whose hands were still tied behind their backs. 'Don't stumble,' was all he said to them, and went back around to the spring-seat. As he kicked off the rear binders the horse leaned into its collar.

The land, which looked flat, was bumpy until

they got away from the vale, got clear of the twin hillocks and were crossing open country. Out there, the land was less rough. Sam looped the lines around the brake-handle to roll and light a smoke. He was unlooping the lines before he made his decision. It was shorter, and therefore quicker, to head for the Pine Cone yard. Rochester would be many additional miles away. He was thinking of the woman. In a day or two someone could take her into town, but for now she needed something softer than a wagon-bed.

He looked over his shoulder. Dusk was down with nightfall close behind. In that uncertain light Baker had slit Mister Beam's trouserleg and was expertly fashioning a pair of splints out of what appeared to be the legs of a cooking tripod. Mister Beam was lying there with a sweaty face staring straight up with his jaws locked. His range riders were watching. They did not look much better, particularly Cotton Buford.

But the evening was cool, which was a blessing, and the horse was having no difficulty now that they were crossing flat country. Abel Carnes and the *vaquero* were likewise having no difficulty. Buford probably would have collapsed, but the tophand and Morales had not been injured. That was why Sam had left Buford in the wagon.

The walking prisoners saw Sam looking back.

122

Neither of them made a sound although they were both thirsty again.

Two miles along Sam halted at the distant sound of riders. He had an idea who that would be, and did not move until the sounds had faded out northward. When the sounds died away he talked up the horse and continued toward Pine Cone, speculating about the reasons Marshal Hedrich had taken so long to get up here. Not that it mattered and in fact he was pleased to have been able to avoid the marshal and his town possemen.

They had the cookhouse light in sight by the time full darkness arrived, and that was a welcome view; Sam had not eaten in a long while. His shoulder no longer pained him with the sharp intensity it had several hours before, but it ached. So did his head and his ribs. With the exception of Carnes and Morales, and Ronald Baker, they were all in pain of one kind or another.

He let the horse pick its way down into the yard and set the brakes over in front of the barn. Upon the porch of his cookhouse, Harold watched them arrive, then ran back inside for a lantern.

CHAPTER THIRTEEN

COLT

Sam untied the arms of Carnes and Morales, then stood regarding them. They did not look very well by lantern light, but then neither did Sam Bolt. He pulled the sixgun from his waistband which he had taken from Cotton Buford and held it out.

Neither the tophand nor the *vaquero* reached out. Sam let the gun hang at his side. 'You couldn't beat me anyway,' he told them. 'Morales, go roll your blankets then go over to the house and tell Mister Beam I said to pay you off.'

The *vaquero* did not speak nor nod his head in understanding. Sam waited, then said, 'I gave you an order.'

Juan Morales finally nodded, very slightly and very gently. 'I'll go. I want to tell you—I was wrong. I was very wrong. Your father was right; a man who does not think does not have any brains.'

Abel spoke up. 'It wasn't him, it was Mister Beam. When you work for a brand, you work for the boss. You want me to quit too?'

Sam leaned down on the tie-rack. He hurt, he was indignant, and he needed another jolt of

124

whiskey just to be able to make it to the cookhouse when Harold beat the triangle to signify he had a meal prepared. And he was also feeling vindictive, which he recognised in himself. He cleared his throat. 'All right,' he said, grudgingly but honestly. 'Beam was wrong and you were idiots ... Maybe right now I'm not actin' much better ... Stay, then.'

'And you?' asked Abel.

Sam spat. 'I'll saddle up in the morning. Pine Cone is a good ranch run by an old bastard.'

'Give him a chance,' Morales said quietly, staring steadily at Bolt. 'This is how he has always lived. All right! today you broke him to lead—you done that to all of us. Tomorrow it will never be the same at Pine Cone ... Sam, I guess if you don't stay, I won't either.'

Bolt pushed up off the rack and turned in the direction of the bunkhouse, but never got there because the *cocinero* came forth to beat on his triangle. Sam turned back and followed in the wake of Buford, Carnes and Morales.

Inside, Harold was like a mother hen. He was bursting with questions which instinct told him not to ask, so instead he fed them until they could hold no more, then, finally, as Sam arose and walked out, Harold turned on Morales and the tophand, but they did not want to talk either, which left the cook standing in his doorway watching as they went over to free the horse and care for it, while Sam Bolt walked

125

over to the porch of the lighted main-house and shoved his way inside without bothering to knock.

He went down a dingy hallway, glanced past an opened door, saw Mister Beam lying out full length atop a large old four-poster bed. Their eyes met and Sam continued on toward the next lighted room.

Baker's wife was finally, at long last, comfortable in a large bed with covers over her and a decent pillow for her head. She was sound asleep.

Baker arose and tiptoed out to Sam. They went along to the parlour and Sam found a decanter of malt whiskey in a glass-fronted cupboard. He filled two glasses in silence and handed one to Baker, then he said, 'In the morning when I head for town I'll rout up the doctor and send him out here.' He sipped the whiskey. It was good quality liquor. He did not take his eyes off the tall man. 'Now I want a straight answer from you, Mister Baker: Who shot old Beam's foreman?'

The thin man had not raised his glass. He met Sam's gaze without difficulty, but he did not speak for so long that Sam was about convinced he had no intention of speaking. Then he said, 'Her brother.'

Sam finished the liquor and put the glass atop a massive oak mantel. 'Tell me the rest of it. Why did he shoot him?'

126

'His name was Colton. We called him Colt. I guess they had called him that since he was a little boy.'

'I don't care what folks called him, Mister Baker. Why did he kill ...?' Sam stopped speaking, his eyes widening. 'Just a minute. What was her brother's last name?'

'Whitson.'

Sam said, 'Damn ... Was he—did he have galloping consumption too?'

'Yes.'

Sam went to a chair and sat down. 'Go on,' he told the taller man, but Baker took his untouched glass to the mantel and placed it up there without speaking. Not until he turned and faced Sam Bolt again. Then all he said was, 'You've figured it out. I can see it in your face.'

Sam's brows dropped slightly. 'But why, for Chris'sake; a man don't shoot his own father.'

Baker also went to a chair. The only light in the dingy big old room was on a small table beside him. He leaned forward clasping his hands and looking steadily over at Sam Bolt. 'Some do, Mister Baker. Some do, if they've had a canker eating inside them ever since they were big enough to understand what he had done to them, to their mother ... Charley Whitson said he would marry their mother ... She died three years back ... in the nation. She died of consumption. She was In'ian. I don't think Whitson ever meant to marry her. The

127

last time she saw him, she came here and they met on the range somewhere. She had Margerie's brother behind the saddle of her old father, and she was carrying my wife. They were to be sent to the nation the following week, unless someone would help them. He gave her thirteen dollars and said it wasn't his fault, then he rode away ... They were sent in boxcars to Indian Territory. Margerie was born down there. Her mother was frail and ailing after that, until she died, and both the children had it too ... Colt was more like their mother; he was In'ian. He looked and thought In'ian ... After I married Margerie I kept him with us while I did some mining and freighting, whatever I could. Colt never talked much, but then when we were going to head south for the desert country where they would both do better, so everyone told me anyway, and came through the Portales country, he came out where I was cookin' supper one night with his guns and told me he was going to die in a few years, but before he got as sick as his sister was, he was going to make good on a promise he had made to himself over his mother's grave ... There isn't a hell of a lot left to tell you, Mister Bolt.'

Sam went over to refill his glass. As he was returning to the chair he gazed at the other man. 'Where is he now?'

'I don't know. I didn't know that he had killed his father until I was buying supplies in the general store at Rochester ... I loaded up that night and headed for the nearest cover ... those foothills where we met. I was going to drive west and circle far around, then head south again, but my horse died. You know the rest of it.'

Sam sat down and winced when his sore shoulder bumped the chair-back. He considered the glass in his hand. He had nothing to say and did not believe that in fact there was much more to be said anyway. He drained the glass and blew his breath out. He wanted a smoke but since it hurt to use his left hand and he'd never mastered the art of rolling cigarettes one-handed, as some rangemen did, he pushed the desire out of his mind.

After a while he said, 'The law will find him, Mister Baker.'

'I suppose so, Mister Bolt, but I hope not. In a couple more years he will be as bad off as my wife is. I'd like to think he'll die at peace, not at the end of a rope or in a prison.'

Sam said, 'I guess so.' He got to his feet, and discovered that he'd taken on more liquor than he should have. Over at the door he turned and said, 'I'll get that damned doctor out here tomorrow if I got to carry him on my back. Good night ... keep her warm.'

Outside, the cookhouse was still lighted, and there was another light at the bunkhouse. He headed in that direction.

Cotton Buford was out back at the wash-rack gingerly cleansing his swollen face. Morales and Abel Carnes were sitting at the old bunkhouse table with a bottle between them, saying nothing. They looked up as Sam entered, and Morales held out the bottle. Sam shook his head and went to a far bunk, kicked off his boots, shed his gunbelt, sank down and turned his back toward the light.

Abel looked at the *vaquero*. Morales shrugged and spoke softly. 'He don't look any better than that lady looks.'

Carnes said nothing. He did not understand much about what had happened today, but of one thing he was certain. 'Tom Hedrich will show up tomorrow. I been thinking about that. There's a lot I don't know, Juan, and I expect there's a lot I never will know, but as far as I'm concerned, it's not my affair and I'm not goin' to tell Tom a damned thing.'

Morales pushed the bottle away. 'How will you do that? He knows something is wrong; if he camps up there until daylight he'll find plenty of sign of trouble. When he comes down here . . .'

'I don't give a damn,' said the tophand, pushing slowly upright. 'He can think what he wants, he's not going to get a blessed word out of me.'

Morales considered the bottle, then arose without reaching for it. He was filthy, bone-

130

tired and troubled. He had been called names today he would ordinarily have tried to kill a man over. He had taken it all without a murmur. Sam Bolt had been right all the way. Morales looked across the table and said, 'Yeah. I don't say anything either . . . Abel, I'm almost forty years old. I never figured I was smart, but I never thought I was a damned fool either. I was wrong . . . Good night.'

The last light to be doused down in the yard was over at the cookshack where Harold put water in a large kettle and laid out his kindling for the morning. He would ordinarily have been tired, but aggravated curiosity kept him wide awake, and later, when he finally did go to his leanto quarters out back, he still was not sleepy.

One light burned all night. That was over at the main-house where Ronald Baker sat on a rickety old ladder-back chair in Mister Beam's room. The older man's leg was swollen. He felt ill and old. He looked steadily at the tall man in the ladder-back chair and said, 'You know how long he worked for me? Well, it don't matter, but he was a friend as well as the best rangeboss we ever had on Pine Cone.'

Baker sat in silence, tired all the way through but unwilling to leave the room. He had told Mister Beam exactly what he had told Sam Bolt. As a result of that, he was drained dry.

Jake Beam's bloodshot eyes roamed the ceiling. They focused well; in fact they were

131

bright again. He said, 'I'll tell you something, Mister Baker, I only told one other man. I saw ... I was sittin' my horse on a hill and saw Charley talk to an In'ian woman who had an old man with her. He had a little kid behind his saddle. I saw Charley give her something—money I thought it was—then he left them sitting there and rode on back where the gather was.'

Jake Beam dropped his eyes to the tall man's face. 'Gawd-damn,' he said softly. 'Charley ... I expect you'd better get in there and see to your wife, Mister Baker ...' The blue-grey eyes swung and as Baker reached the doorway Mister Beam also said, 'I'll get the doctor from town out here.'

Baker nodded, his face almost expressionless except for that faint look of pain Sam had noticed.

'One other thing, Mister Baker ... The lawman over at Rochester is damned good at his trade. He'll find her brother. That's between the pair of us, not to be told to her.'

Baker raised a hand to the doorframe gazing back at the older man. 'Maybe. I hope not ... And I think he won't. Colt's all In'ian. You don't find them unless they want you to ... There are a lot of mountains around this country, Mister Beam.' Baker continued to stand there a few moments longer before he said, 'You'd hang him, wouldn't you?'

132

Jake Beam's eyes wavered. Instead of offering a direct answer he said, 'Mister Baker, I hope to gawd you're never in the position I'm in right now. Good night.'

After Baker went along to his wife's room the old man continued to gaze up where lamplight made a series of filigreed shadow-patterns on the ceiling. He did not go to sleep for a long time, and when he finally did, it was because emotional exhaustion more than physical exhaustion demanded it of his bruised and aged body.

There was no moon, and those sifting high clouds Sam Bolt had noticed the day before came stealthily in the night to form a high lattice over the immense curve of heaven. Stars looked moist and obscure, the air had a different smell and taste to it.

Somewhere to the west a wolf sounded, and moments later got his answer. It was past mating time, and the reply he had got was from a bitch swollen with young, but wolves were gregarious creatures, they could not be alone, not even toothless old lobos with cropped ears and worm-distended bellies. But those calls had been made by young wolves who could silently course the night until they met, then go farther off into the mountains to start digging one of the big dens the bitch would require when her time came. They would make several such dens. The one she whelped in would get foul soon enough, and her new companion would help her take the pups one at a time to the new and cleaner den.

Before dawn the promise of rain was heavy. Harold went out back to fling away his basin of shaving water, and stopped out there to wrinkle his nose, then lift his eyes. It had not occurred to him, or to anyone else at Pine Cone, that rain was on the way.

Not that he objected. Old Tatum had been a rangeman most of his life. He welcomed rain the same way he welcomed springtime. It belonged and he belonged, and without rain there would be nothing.

He returned to the stove and generously sifted in oatmeal while vigorously stirring the kettle full of boiling water. It was a matter of pride that a cook did not serve the stuff with lumps in it, although he had yet to hear a hungry rangerider complain about lumps—nor bad coffee, nor for that matter, a lot of other things.

CHAPTER FOURTEEN

THE DAY AFTER

Mister Beam sent for Sam Bolt before he'd had his breakfast, and when Sam walked in the old man was sitting on the edge of his bed shaving, his splinted leg shoved out like a log. He looked at the man in the doorway and said, 'Harold's goin' to fetch over some coffee . . . I won't keep you long, you'll be hungry.' He motioned with the straight-razor. 'Have a chair.'

Sam went over and sat down as Mister Beam rinsed off and towelled his face, then hoisted his leg and settled into a sitting position on the bed. Sam said, 'How is the leg this morning?'

Mister Beam's answer was forthright. 'Better than it was yesterday. That feller knows how to splint broken bones.'

Sam had got the civilities out of the way and sat in silence, waiting for Mister Beam to say whatever was on his mind. It was not a very long wait. 'I know who killed Charley. I guess he told you the same story.'

Sam nodded, still silent.

'I don't know what to say, Mister Bolt.'

Sam was no help at all. He regarded the older man steadily without opening his mouth.

Mister Beam's eyes wavered. 'Well; being wrong isn't just peculiar to me, only I couldn't sleep last night, so I had a long time to punish myself. You were right and no one would listen.'

Sam leaned back, crossing his legs, and felt uncomfortable because he knew how bitterly hard it was for a man like Jake Beam to humiliate himself.

'I don't know where her brother is . . . Hedrich will most likely find him . . . I sort of

135

hope he don't ... I think we'd better keep Missus Baker here where she can get good care ... What do you think of her husband?'

'Good man ... Better than the sons of bitches who would have murdered him yesterday, Mister Beam.'

For a moment Jake Beam was silent. His colour brightened and his eyes hardened. He struggled in silence for a while then spoke again in the same controlled tone of voice. 'Maybe ... What I meant was, do you expect he'd be any good on a cow outfit?'

Sam's instincts told him something was coming; told him that Mister Beam was not entirely concerned with keeping Baker on Pine Cone. 'You can find out right easy,' he replied. 'If he don't work out, fire him.'

'Well no, Mister Bolt, I couldn't do that. We got his wife to think about. But he strikes me as a man who maybe hasn't worked cattle a lot, only he'd learn. He's handy for a fact. Look at that splint.'

Sam did not look at the splint, he was thinking of those sticks of dynamite. 'He's handy. Try him. I expect he'll make you a darned good man.'

'... You care to tell him we'd like to hire him on?'

Their eyes held for a long time. 'Who is *we*, Mister Beam?'

'You an' me ... Charley's gone, Abel would

never take the rangeboss job.'

'How do you know I'd be any good at it?'

Old Beam's thin lips drew up slightly and his gaze was sardonic. 'I been handling men all my life, Sam. I've yet to make a mistake in hiring one for the ranch.'

Sam arose from the chair. 'Mister Beam, you are a mean old son of a bitch. You wouldn't change ... But thanks for making the offer anyway.'

Sam walked out into the hallway and nearly collided with Harold who was carrying a tray with coffee and two cups on it. Sam went out front, crossed the yard and entered the cookshack where Cotton Buford was lingerng over his coffee, having already finished eating. Morales and Carnes were gone, their places marked only by empty plates and cups. Sam piled a plate at the stove and went to the table. As he sat down he could feel Cotton's pale eyes on him and raised his head.

Cotton's face was swollen on one side but his eyes were clear, so evidently if he had pain it was not a constant thing. He tried to smile at Sam Bolt. 'Still got hard feelings?' he asked, and as Sam got settled at the table and raised his eyes, it was easy to read the light-haired man's expression. Cotton was a guileless individual. Sam shook his head and raised his knife and fork. Cotton said, 'Me neither ... I'll tell you something, Sam; you scairt the whey out of me yesterday.'

Sam spoke around his breakfast. 'Forget it, Cotton.'

The cowboy nodded slightly. 'Yeah ... Maybe in another few days ... You sure set Pine Cone on its ear. Even old Harold's goin' around like a chicken with its head cut off.'

Sam continued to eat, and the *cocinero* came in hurrying from out back. He saw Sam Bolt and blurted out words. 'Horsemen, looks like four or five. Coming toward the yard frm the north.' He paused, looking straight at Sam. 'The feller out front is Marshal Hedrich.'

Sam went on eating. Cotton waited, and when nothing more was said, he arose and limped out of the cookshack. The moment the door closed Harold came over and spoke swiftly in a lowered tone. 'I went after him yestiddy, like you said.'

Sam looked up. 'Like Mister Beam told you to do.'

'Well, yes, but I was fixin' to go anyway, like you said.' Harold fidgeted. 'Jesus; this is a hell of a fix.' Sam arose to go after more coffee and returned to continue eating. Harold went to the door and stood there a while, then came back. 'He's about a quarter-mile out.'

Sam picked up his empty plate and cup, took them to the large wash-pan which held other breakfast dishes in greasy water, then turned toward the door. Harold said, 'Stay in here. He'll want to see Mister Beam. No sense in you

138

goin' out there.'

Sam let the door close after himself and went down off the porch and across to the barn. He saw the horsemen. They were riding at a flat walk, clearly in no hurry. He went down through the barn and out back to look at his horse. Someone had forked in a bait of hay. The horse acknowledged his presence by blowing its nose and briefly watching, then dropped its head and resumed eating.

Sam built a smoke and was turning back when Abel Carnes came up and nodded. 'Did you see who's coming?'

Sam lit up nodding his head.

'Juan and Cotton and me got nothing at all to tell him. Nothing.'

Sam considered the dark-eyed, lanky man while trickling blue smoke, then walked past up through the barn and out front where the hitch-rack was, and leaned there in the warm but dull and overcast morning waiting for Hedrich to reach the yard. He had known Tom Hedrich a long time.

Morales appeared over on the small porch of the bunkhouse, mahogany-coloured and poker-faced. He leaned on an upright with one hand resting on the saw-handle of his holstered Colt. Sam studied him for a while then called up there. 'Go take off that damned gunbelt.'

Morales did not move at once, but he moved before the possemen entered the yard, and reappeared later without his weapon.

Tom Hedrich had a blanketroll behind his cantle. He had not shaved yet, and was bundled inside a canvas coat with blanket lining. The men with him were not strangers to Sam. One was Frank English's helper at the smithy in town. Another worked as a clerk at the general store. The other two were rangemen. Tom had probably scooped them up at the cafe or the saloon and brought them along. Sam knew them both because he had been tophand until six months ago for the ranch they still rode for.

Marshal Hedrich still took his time. As he approached the rack he studied all the buildings and the big yard in general. He was packing a saddlegun. So were the men behind him. When he turned toward the rack his gaze met the gaze of Sam Bolt. Hedrich said, 'Morning, Sam.'

Bolt nodded. ''Morning, Tom.'

As Hedrich dismounted he glanced toward the main-house. 'Mister Beam over there?'

Sam nodded, and returned the nods of the possemen as they also swung off and looped their reins. Marshal Hedrich hesitated, glanced again toward the main-house, unbuttoned his coat and jerked his head. 'Let's walk out back,' he said, and turned to lead the way, leaving his possemen with their animals in front of the barn.

Alone beside the corral which held Sam's horse, Hedrich turned and said, 'What in the

140

hell went on up yonder?'

'A misunderstanding,' replied Bolt.

Hedrich's steady eyes were fixed on Sam. 'Yeah; blew holes in those little hills. I'd say it was some misunderstanding. Sam . . .'

'Wait a minute, Tom. I forgot to thank you for sending me out to see about that foreman's job.'

Hedrich fidgeted slightly and glanced around at the eating horse.

'I been in the Portales country two seasons now, so maybe I should have heard about Jake Beam. But I never did. But you did; you knew what kind of a man he was.'

'What do you mean? He's big in these parts, runs lots of . . .'

'Tom, you knew when you sent me out here he was a first-class old son of a bitch.'

Hedrich protested. 'Wait a minute, damn it all, Sam. He's no tougher nor different than all the other mossbacks in the West. Hell, you didn't come down in the last rain; you've run into his kind before.'

'But not when they're out lookin' for blood.'

'Well, I didn't know all . . .'

'Yes you did, Tom. You knew he was tryin' to find the man who shot his rangeboss.'

'Well . . .'

'Tom, you go on in there and talk to that old bastard. I think he's goin' to tell you quite a story.'

'You mean lie to me?'

Sam snorted. 'No. He's not going to lie to you. If you know so much about those old mossbacks you know they wouldn't lie to save their souls ... He's going to give you an earful you don't expect. As for the man who bushwhacked his rangeboss ...'

'Hold it, Sam ... One question: Anyone get shot up bad or killed up yonder where the fight took place?'

'Not shot up and not killed, but hurt a little. Old Beam's flat on his back with a busted leg. Some of the rest of us got lumps and aches.'

'Good,' stated Marshal Hedrich, showing an expression of great relief. 'That worried me all the way down here this morning ... I got the man who shot Charley Whitson. I was scairt pea-green after what Harold told me that Mister Beam was going to lynch Ronald Baker, and he didn't have anything to do with the bushwhacking.'

Sam was staring. 'You got the bushwhacker?'

'Yeah.'

'What did he tell you?'

'Nothing. He's sick. Some freighters found him lying beside the south road with his horse standing over him. They brought 'em both into town.'

'What's his name?'

'Colton Whitson. Does that last name surprise you, Sam?'

'No. How do you know he shot old Beam's rangeboss?'

'He told Henry Lord when the freighters left him with doc. Henry told me.'

Sam sighed. 'You better go up and see Mister Beam.'

'Yeah,' Marshal Hedrich murmured, looking at Sam Bolt. 'Is there something else?'

Sam nodded slowly. 'Yeah. Mister Beam can tell you.' He turned away and entered the barn from out back and halted at the saddle pole to lean there gazing up into the yard where that gunmetal-coloured daylight made visibility clear enough, but without shadows.

He was still down there when Baker entered the barn and came over to say, 'I been looking for you.'

Sam raised just his face. 'You found me.'

'About that doctor in town . . .'

Sam straightened up. It crossed his mind instantly that Baker should not go to town to seek the doctor. 'I'll go right now,' he said.

Baker nodded, evidently accepting that. Then he said, 'I passed the marshal heading for the house.'

Sam leaned on a saddle. 'Mister Beam will tell him everything . . . I expect he'll want to talk to you and your wife.' He gazed at the tall man; he did not want to tell him that his wife's brother had been found and arrested. Somebody would tell him, perhaps soon now, but Sam did not want to be the one. 'I'll saddle up.' He turned back toward the rear of the barn and Baker gazed after him wearing a quizzical expression. There had been something on Bolt's mind which was troubling him; that was obvious. Baker decided not to press it because he did not believe he would make much headway, so he turned to leave the barn, and passed Abel Carnes at the doorway. They nodded and Abel went on through and out back where Sam was opening the corral gate. He said, 'Morales rode for Doctor Lord.'

Sam turned away from the horse. He had not wanted to make that ride anyway. He and the tophand returned to the barn and Abel wagged his head. 'You're makin' a mistake,' he said, and Sam halted to look around. 'About what?'

Abel faced Bolt. 'About not takin' the foreman's job.'

'You been talkin' to Mister Beam?'

'Yes. He told me to talk to you about it. Sam, try it—make it work. Let me tell you something; I've worked for Pine Cone a long time. But yesterday and today have changed a whole hell of a lot of things. I don't want the job, couldn't do it as well as you and Charley could do it. You made things change. If you ride away a lot of things will have been for nothing.'

'Nothing will ever change Mister Beam, Abel.'

'Yeah, something will, and right now he's up

144

to his gullet in it. Age for one thing, an awful close call over hanging the wrong man, and I think most of all, getting whipped to a frazzle by someone who don't quit when he knows he's right. You don't know Mister Beam as well as I do, Sam. Take the job. He'll listen to you. He knows he'd better listen to you.'

Sam almost smiled at the dark-eyed man. 'Abel, you ever think about preaching?'

Carnes returned the smile. 'Never did ... I'll tell you somethin' else. That woman in there is dying. No matter what Doc Lord does, she's goin' on her way ... Well; Mister Beam's got knots in his guts over that too. Charley was more than his foreman, he was also his friend. The old man's lyin' in there staring at the damned ceiling up to his hocks in something he don't know how to handle—and that lady is going to die on him.'

CHAPTER FIFTEEN

SAM'S DECISION

Abel was right, but it had been no secret to anyone who had seen Margerie Baker, and after Doctor Lord came and went, and Mister Beam hobbled to the parlour to see the man he had sent for, with a light rain falling out in the yard,

145

she died holding her husband's hand, and as they talked in the parlour in measured tones, neither knew that the only real travail which never made a sound had come and gone.

Mister Beam said, 'Sam; I been all my life with livestock and open country, and not always with very many people. I think someone has decided it's time for Jacob Beam to learn a lesson an' maybe bleed at the heart a little ... Hedrich told you he's got Charley's killer. He didn't tell you Whitson is dying... It makes me sick thinkin' how bad I wanted to kill him. You know what it was? I never tried to listen to anyone else. I just wanted to make the only law I know work like it was supposed to work. Like it worked for my paw and his paw, and right on down to me ... Young Whitson is goin' to die soon. Henry Lord told Tom Hedrich that... There's whiskey in the sideboard if you'd care for some.'

Sam did not move.

'You don't want the foreman's job. Well; that bothers me too, but it's not my decision. You'll ride on, I expect. What I'm tryin' to tell you is that ... I never had anyone face me down and be right all the way and I was wrong all the way. I guess that's all I wanted to say.'

Sam arose, now, and filled two glasses and returned to hand Mister Beam one and take the other glass back to the chair with him. 'What about Hedrich?' he asked, raising the glass.

146

'He's goin' back to town.'

'That's all?'

'I told him what happened up yonder. He said it would be up to Mister Baker if he wanted to make a complaint... He didn't. He told Tom it was a mistake, an' that was all it was.'

Sam sipped whiskey, and raised his eyes to the doorway of the dingy hall when Ronald Baker came soundlessly to lean there. Sam's stomach knotted. Baker said, 'She is gone.'

For a long time no one spoke, then Jake Beam twisted to look around. 'There's a Bible on my dresser, Mister Baker. I'll join you in a minute.' He turned toward Sam again and put aside his untouched glass. He did not speak and the pain in his gunmetal eyes moved Sam to put his own glass aside and arise to leave the house.

Outside, each raindrop was like a tear. Sam went to the barn to be alone for a while. He had not really known her, unless it was possible to know someone who was naturally good just in passing. He felt pain over her loss as though he had known her a long time.

Morales came in out of the rain, saw Sam and came over. 'They'll never hang the bushwhacker,' he said. 'I saw him at the doctor's place. He's nothing but sinew and will-power. The doctor said maybe a week, maybe three weeks.'

Sam gazed at the Mexican for a moment. 'Juan; the lady died a little while ago.'

147

Morales's eyes widened, then he crossed himself and said in his native language, 'May it be known to God that she has fulfilled His will on earth. Maybe she knows peace and beauty forever.'

'Juan; when the rain lets up we'll make a place in the cemetery out yonder. She can lie near the rangeboss.' He thought a moment. 'And her brother, he can lie out there too.'

Morales did not question the idea of burying Whitson beside the man he had killed, who had been his father. Maybe Morales had not heard that they had been father and son, but he did know they had the same name, and Morales was not a fool.

He stepped to the saddle-pole for support. 'I passed the marshal and his riders.'

Sam felt the question in those words. 'It's finished. No one was killed up there, or Hedrich would not have left the yard without prisoners.'

'Do you wonder why things work out the way they do?'

Sam shook his head. 'No . . . When the rain stops we'll make a grave . . . What were you doing around here before all this happened?'

'Doing? We were going to make a gather, cull down, make a shipment and trail it over to the railroad siding beyond . . .'

'I know where the siding is. There's got to be at least two more riders.'

Morales was looking closely at Sam Bolt now.

148

'Yes. At least two. Maybe three, for a while, because Cotton's not goin' to be able to work hard for another week or so.'

Sam said, 'Harold?' and the *vaquero's* dark eyes shone sardonically. 'No. Once maybe, but no longer. Besides, if he had to leave his flour barrels...' Morales shrugged.

'Flour barrels?'

'He's got bottles of whiskey hidden in the flour barrels. Harold don't work very well without his medicine. Everyone knows it but Mister Beam. He don't allow whiskey very much on Pine Cone.'

'You got it in the bunkhouse, Juan.'

'Not when he's in there, Sam.'

'I guess I'll talk to him about two more men.'

Morales softly nodded as though to confirm something to himself. 'You stay,' he said quietly.

'For a while anyway, Juan.'

Morales left the barn and Sam rolled and lit a smoke, then stood a long while in the doorway of the barn listening to rain on the roof and watching it out across the yard. It was a late spring rain, warm and light and life-carrying.

Photoset, printed and bound in Great Britain by REDWOOD BURN LIMITED, Trowbridge, Wiltshire